Fa la la la Felt

Fa la la la Felt

45 Handmade Holiday Decorations

AMANDA CARESTIO

LARK

New York

Editor:
KATHY SHELDON

Art Director:
SUSAN WASINGER

Illustrator:
ORRIN LUNDGREN

Photographer:
SUSAN WASINGER

Cover Designer:
SUSAN WASINGER

New York

An Imprint of Sterling Publishing Co., Inc.
1166 Avenue of the Americas
New York, NY 10036

ISBN 978-1-60059-615-5

Library of Congress Cataloging-in-Publication Data

Carestio, Amanda.
  Fa la la la felt : 45 handmade holiday decorations / Amanda Carestio. -- 1st ed.
    p. cm.
  Includes index.
  ISBN 978-1-60059-615-5 (pb-pbk. : alk. paper)
  1. Felt work. 2. Christmas decorations. I. Title.
  TT849.5.C37 2010
  746'.0463--dc22

                    2009045037

Distributed in Canada by Sterling Publishing Co., Inc.
c/o Canadian Manda Group, 664 Annette Street
Toronto, Ontario M6S 2C8, Canada
Distributed in the United Kingdom by GMC Distribution Services
Castle Place, 166 High Street, Lewes, East Sussex BN7 1XU, England
Distributed in Australia by NewSouth Books
45 Beach Street, Coogee NSW 2034, Australia

For information about custom editions, special sales, and premium and corporate purchases, please contact Sterling Special Sales at 800-805-5489 or specialsales@sterlingpublishing.com.

Manufactured in China

10 12 14 16 18 20 19 17 15 13 11

sterlingpublishing.com
larkcrafts.com

Contents

Merry, crafty & bright

WHEN IT COMES TO THE HOLIDAYS, people tend to fall into two categories. You're a domestic holiday goddess—with homemade gifts, made-from-scratch treats, and hand-lettered cards galore—or a mistress of the last-minute, wrapping gifts on the way from the store to your in-laws' house. Okay, I'll admit it: Despite my best intentions, I tend to fall into the making-gifts-at-midnight-on-Christmas-Eve category. And I'll admit something else: Felt is not my usual cup of tea.

But recently I've fallen in love with felt: how simple it is to stitch because it doesn't ravel when cut, how it makes the perfect canvas for embroidery, and the way it seems to magically transform into the most adorable projects. As I began to notice designers from places as far-flung as Australia, the UK, and Portugal all making beautiful felt creations, I knew I wanted to gather them together in a book to show how fresh felt could look for Christmas. And I was delighted to discover that crafting with felt can be green: Everyone seems to be experimenting with earth-friendly felt, from eco-felt (made from recycled plastic bottles) to bamboo felt and recycled felted sweater material.

In *Fa la la la Felt,* you'll find 45 handmade ornaments, decorations, and stockings. Want classic Christmas colors and themes? See the Sorta Swedish stockings on page 114 or the Christmas Candy Garland on page 80. Is your flavor of fa la la la more indie and inventive? Deck your halls with Holiday Toadstools (page 28) or hang Three Wise Fish (page 34) on your tree. Need an ornament that's both pretty and purposeful? Try Sew Merry (page 36), an ornament that doubles as a pincushion in the off-season. Want to admire your handiwork year-round? Made with subtle hues that go with any season, the Little Birds Garland (page 77) may be for you. And when you've created a few projects, make the most of your colorful leftovers with the Scrap Wreath (page 82), which doesn't require a single stitch—even better.

Bye bye, excuses. Hello, domestic holiday goddess! Put on some Christmas carols, make some hot cocoa, grab some felt, and… get crafty!

Felt Basics

If you sew at all, you probably already have most of what you need to make the projects in this book, and you'll just have to buy the felt and a few embellishments. Of course, nothing is more frustrating than getting three-quarters of the way through a project and realizing you don't have the one thing you need to finish it, so read through this Basics section (and the project you're making) quickly to make sure you're all set before you get started. Along with materials and tools needed, you'll also find a quick primer on any special techniques our designers used when making the projects.

Basic Materials

FELT

If you haven't worked with felt before, you're going to love it. It's easy to cut, sew, and embellish, and it doesn't fray. (How can you not love a fabric that doesn't fray?) It's perfect for beginning sewers or even kids, but the felt available now is so attractive that skilled crafters are creating beautiful works with it.

If your last experience with felt was back in grade school, prepare to be delighted. These days, you can find hand-dyed wool felt, wool/rayon felt, 100 percent acrylic felt, eco-felt made from post-consumer recycled plastic bottles, and even felt made from bamboo and rayon. A few of the projects in this book also call for felted material (fabric from wool sweaters that have been purposely shrunk). See the sidebar on page 8 for simple sweater felting instructions. For the most part, you can use whichever kind of felt you prefer for your Christmas projects, but the different types do offer advantages and disadvantages.

WOOL FELT One hundred percent wool is the thickest felt. It's the sturdiest, it hides needle holes and seams best, and it won't open up at the stitch holes when you stuff projects. You can dye wool felt or purchase it in beautiful and subtle hand-dyed colors. It won't tear apart or pill the way acrylic felt often does. Also—and this is something to consider with Christmas decorations and ornaments—wool felt is less flammable than acrylic felt. But you can't machine wash or dry wool felt, it costs more than acrylic, and it's harder to find at your local big box craft store (you can, however, find plenty of wool felt online).

WOOL/RAYON FELT Wool/rayon felt is very similar to 100 percent wool felt. The addition of rayon makes the felt more flexible, so it's easier to sew and drapes a little better than pure wool felt. Wool/rayon felt is less expensive than wool felt but more than acrylic felt.

ACRYLIC FELT Acrylic felt is made by pressing tiny acrylic fibers until they interlock into a mat of material. Its benefits are that it is inexpensive, widely available, fade resistant, and able to be machine washed and dried. But acrylic felt is also usually thinner—and therefore more transparent—than wool felt. It also stretches out of shape more easily, tends to gape and open up at stitch holes (especially in stuffed projects), and gets fuzzy if handled a lot.

Color Your Cloth

Felt comes in colors that cover the spectrum from subtly sophisticated to terrifically tacky. It's available at craft stores as sheets or off bolts. Or look online for even more color options, including felt from talented fabric designers like Heather Bailey.

Creating Felted Fabric

A few of the projects in this book call for felted fabric (although you can substitute felted fabric for commercial felt as desired). Felting fabric is essentially just doing something we've all done by accident—shrinking a wool sweater—on purpose. Here's how:

1. Start with a 100 percent wool sweater (one the moths have been munching or a thrift-store find).

2. Place your sweater in a zippered lingerie bag or a pillow protector (otherwise, you'll have a lot of wet lint to clean out of your washing machine, and trust me, you'd rather be crafting).

3. Set your washer to the hot wash/cold rinse cycle, and use the lowest water level setting and the longest cycle. Add about one tablespoon of mild dish soap or wool wash.

4. If the sweater shrinks as desired, hang it to dry. If you want more shrinkage, wash it again and then dry it in your dryer. The end result should be soft felted fabric that won't ravel when cut.

ECO FELT Made from post-consumer plastic bottles, eco felt shares almost all of acrylic felt's characteristics, but it is, of course, reusing something that might otherwise clog the landfills. One added benefit of acrylic and eco felt is that they are preferred by people who are allergic to wool or averse to using products that come from animals.

BAMBOO FELT Very new on the scene is bamboo felt. Super soft, bamboo felt is typically 50 percent bamboo and 50 percent rayon. This makes it a natural, renewable material that is also vegan. Your best place to find bamboo felt at this point is online.

THREAD & FLOSS

It took me a while to learn this but when it comes to thread, just shell out a bit more and get the good stuff. Buy a quality polyester, cotton/polyester blend, or all-cotton thread for machine and hand stitching. It will make sewing much easier and give you strong seams that will stay that way. For decorative embroidery stitches, your best bet is standard embroidery floss, available in tons of different colors at craft and fabric stores. Look on page 10 for illustrations of all the stitches used in this book.

STUFFING

It really doesn't matter what you use to stuff most of these projects. You can use polyester fiberfill, cotton batting, wool roving, or even sewing scraps. You could even add a bit of potpourri (see Snowflake Baubles on page 14), spices, or herbs so your projects look *and* smell good.

EMBELLISHMENTS

The truth is you may already have the embellishments you need to make many of these projects. But if you try hard, you can find just a few things you need to run out and purchase. Who doesn't like shopping for things like ribbon and buttons? They're so pretty, and they don't cost much. Skim through the projects you want to make, and note the embellishments you'll need, such as buttons, beads, or rickrack. Of course, part of the fun of creating is doing your own thing, so feel free to think of the embellishments listed as suggestions and substitute freely.

Basic Tools

You don't need any fancy tools to work with felt. In fact, many of the projects in this book can be made without a sewing machine; look for the no-sew logo. If you don't already have all your tools in one place, take a moment to gather the items in the Basic Sewing Kit at right.

Basic Techniques

Many of the same techniques you use for other sewing projects will work with felt, and in many respects, felt is actually a bit easier to work with than other fabrics.

USING TEMPLATES

You'll find all the templates you need in the back of the book, including pattern pieces, embroidery designs, and info on how to use them (page 116).

FINISHING EDGES

Perhaps the biggest difference between felt and other fabrics—and part of what makes it so great to work with—is how you treat the edges. Since the edges of felt fabric don't fray, you have lots of options for how to finish them, depending on the overall look you're going for.

Basic Sewing Kit

scissors

pinking shears

rotary cutting tools (optional)

straight pins

hand-sewing needle

embroidery needle

sewing machine (optional)

ruler

craft glue (optional)

fabric pen

- For a quick and folksy look, try pinking the edges, as in Holiday Hearts (page 46).

- For a handcrafted edge that takes a little bit more work, blanket stitch over your edges as in the Little Birds Garland (page 77).

- For an "unfinished finish" that's unmistakably handmade, use a straight or running stitch near the edge of the felt and leave the edges raw as in Leaf & Vine Stocking (page 104).

- Or skip the stitching altogether: see the Scrap Wreath on page 82.

Embroidery Stitches

Embroidery stitches are the perfect way to add a little fa la la to your felt projects. As a general guide, most embroidery stitches in this book are created with two or three strands of floss (which will require you to split the floss), though look to the individual project for specific instructions. These illustrations will help you with any unfamiliar stitches.

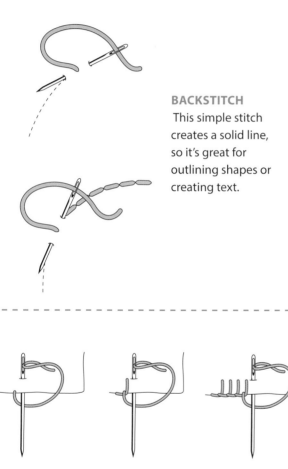

BACKSTITCH This simple stitch creates a solid line, so it's great for outlining shapes or creating text.

BLANKET STITCH The blanket stitch is both decorative and functional. Use this stitch to accentuate an edge or to attach an appliqué.

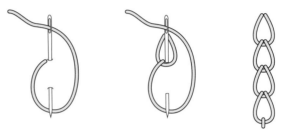

CHAIN STITCH This stitch is perfect when you need a slightly thicker line.

DOUBLE-THREADED RUNNING STITCH This stitch is very similar to the single-threaded running stitch, although it uses two strands of woven floss instead of one.

FRENCH KNOT This elegant little knot adds interest and texture when embroidering or embellishing.

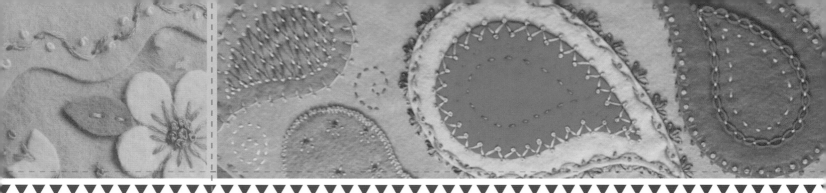

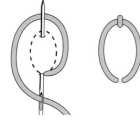

LAZY DAISY Make a small loop and then anchor it with a single stitch at the top for a decorative stitch that resembles a flower petal.

SATIN STITCH
The satin stitch is composed of parallel rows of straight stitches and is often used to fill in an outline.

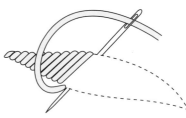

STEM STITCH
This is also known as a crewel stitch and is often used to outline a shape.

RUNNING STITCH
Make this stitch by weaving the needle through the fabric at evenly spaced intervals.

SINGLE-THREADED RUNNING STITCH
This stitch starts with a basic line of running stitches. Then, working on the top of the felt, weave a single length of floss under the stitches to create a wave-like stitch.

WHIPSTITCH Also called the overcast stitch, the whipstitch is used to bind edges to prevent raveling or for decorative purposes. Simply stitch over the edge of the fabric.

Fa la la la ornaments

Whether your tree is green or white or even flocked pink, here are ornaments aplenty to adorn and delight. From charming critters to graphic sym-bols to beaded confections, all it takes is a little felt, a couple of stitches, and a bit of imagination to animate your holidays and light up your tree for years to come.

The dried balsam in these **Snowflake Baubles** will fill your house with Christmas cheer.

Snowflake Baubles

DESIGNER: ESTHER COAR

WHAT YOU NEED

Basic sewing kit (page 9)

Embroidery templates (page 123)

Fusible fleece

Blue flannel print

Light green, light blue, and white felt

Blue and white embroidery floss

Metallic thread

Matching heavy-duty or quilting thread

Stuffing

Dried balsam

WHAT YOU DO

1 Iron the fusible fleece onto the back of the flannel print following the manufacturer's instructions. This will prevent fraying and add thickness to the flannel. Cut the flannel into 5-inch (12.7 cm) squares.

2 Cut the felt into 5-inch (12.7 cm) squares.

3 Transfer the snowflake embroidery templates—including the circle shape—to the felt squares that will make up your ornament fronts. Do not trim the circles.

4 Embroider the motifs with embroidery floss and metallic threads using simple stitches such as backstitch, stem stitch, and French knots. Use two strands of floss and one strand of metallic thread. Now cut out the circle.

5 Place the embroidered circle onto a second felt or flannel square. Using matching thread, sew the layers together. Trim the second layer circle slightly larger than the first embroidered circle. (Don't be a perfectionist! Cutting freehand adds to the homemade look.) Repeat this process until your ornament is the desired size.

6 Place the finished ornament front on a final felt square, and trace it. Mark the tops of both the front and back of the ornament. Cut out the back. Stitch the front and back together, leaving a 1-inch (2.5 cm) hole at the top for the stuffing and the hanger.

7 Fill the ornament with stuffing, inserting a small pocket of balsam down into the center.

8 Stitch the ornament closed, and create a double-stranded hanging loop with the thread.

These Winter Critter Portraits are adorable ornaments, but you could also put a pin on the back of one and call it a brooch.

Winter Critter Portraits

DESIGNER: CATHY GAUBERT

WHAT YOU NEED

(to make the fox)

Basic sewing kit (page 9)

Templates (page 121)

Black wool felt, 5-inch (12.7 cm) square

Red wool felt, 2-inch (5 cm) square

White wool felt, 2-inch (5 cm) square

Aqua wool felt, 4-inch (10.2 cm) square

Red, white, and black thread

White, black, and red embroidery floss

Fabric glue

WHAT YOU DO

1 Use the templates to cut one frame shape and one hat shape from black felt, one body shape from red, and one face shape from white. Using the scallop blade or scissors, cut one portrait shape from aqua.

2 Using the photo as a guide, place the body shape onto the portrait circle, letting the bottom edge hang over. With red thread, stitch just inside the edge of the body. Place the head slightly on top of the body, and stitch it in place with white thread, just inside the edge. Place the hat at an angle on top of the head, and stitch it down with black thread just inside the edge.

3 Turn the portrait over, and cut the body along the bottom edge to match the scalloped border.

4 Using two strands of black embroidery floss, make a French knot for the eye and satin-stitch the nose. With three strands of white floss, make stitches of varying lengths to add dimension to the face. Using two strands of red floss, stipple the body or add other details, such as buttons, a collar, a monogram, a flower (for the hare), or polka dots (for the kitten).

5 With three strands of white embroidery floss, randomly cover the portrait circle background with French knots.

6 Use fabric glue or hand stitching to attach the completed portrait to the black frame.

7 Run a 9-inch (22.9 cm) piece of floss through the top of the frame, and tie the tails together for a hanger.

The blanket-stitched edging on these
little Russian **Matryoshka Dolls**
just adds to their ahh factor.

Matryoshka Dolls

DESIGNER: KAREN DE NARDI

WHAT YOU NEED

(to make the blue & pink doll)

Basic sewing kit (page 9)

Templates (page 124)

Dark pink felt (for the back and body)

Blue adhesive felt (for the headscarf and flower)

Scrap of white felt

Black and pink sewing thread

Scrap of matching floral-patterned fabric

Cream embroidery floss, 36 inches (91.4 cm)

Stuffing

Cream ribbon, 5¹/₂ inches (14 cm)

WHAT YOU DO

1 Using the templates, cut out two body shapes from the dark pink felt and one headscarf and flower shape from the blue adhesive felt. (Note: If you don't have adhesive felt, use regular felt and glue.) Cut one round face shape from white felt, making sure it's slightly larger than the inner circle edge of the headscarf.

2 Place the headscarf right side down. Peel off the adhesive backing paper (or apply fabric glue to the back), and stick the white face piece in position on the back. Then stick the headscarf, with the face added, onto one of the body pieces.

3 Using the photo as a guide, embroider two eyes with black thread, and use small stiches to make eyelashes. Create lips with the pink thread.

4 Cut a small piece of matching cotton fabric to place in the center of the flower. Remove the adhesive backing paper from the flower, stick the cotton fabric in position on the back, and stick the flower onto the doll's belly.

5 Using three strands of cream embroidery floss and starting at the top of the doll's head, begin to blanket-stitch around the doll shape to join the front and back body pieces together.

6 Stop stitching about 1¹/₂ inches (3.8 cm) before you get back to your starting point. Stuff the doll as firmly as desired, and complete the edge stitching. Leave the thread hanging.

7 Attach the ribbon to the back of the head using the remaining thread.

Start a new family tradition by hanging these Christmas Cones. If you've been good all year, maybe Santa will fill them with treats.

Christmas Cones

DESIGNER: ELLEN LUCKETT BAKER

WHAT YOU NEED

(to make one)

Basic sewing kit (page 9)

Template (page 116)

Wool felt, 8 x 8 inches (20.3 x 20.3 cm)

Embroidered ribbon, 26 inches (66 cm)

Matching sewing thread

Blunt tool

WHAT YOU DO

1 Cut one cone shape following the template.

2 Cut a 10-inch (25.4 cm) length of ribbon. Pin and stitch the ribbon along the rounded edge of the felt, sewing just along the top edge. Trim any excess ribbon.

3 Fold the felt in half, with right sides together. Pin and sew along the straight raw edge, using a $1/4$-inch (6 mm) seam allowance. Use an overcast stitch if you'd prefer.

4 Turn right sides out, pushing the tip out with a blunt tool.

5 To make the handle, use the remaining 16 inches (40.6 cm) of ribbon. Fold the ribbon in half, and tuck the ends under to prevent fraying. Pin it to itself, with wrong sides together, and sew along each long edge so the ribbon pattern is on both sides.

6 Pin the handle to the both sides of the cone's top edge, and sew it in place.

These Felt Flora ornaments will
add a pop of cheerful color
to any tree.

Felt Flora

DESIGNER: CATHY ZIEGELE

WHAT YOU NEED

(to make the green ornament)

Basic sewing kit (page 9)

Templates (page 122)

Green, light green, and pink felt

Thin cotton batting

Hole punches, ¼-inch (6 mm) and a smaller one for the hanger hole

Green seed beads

Light green embroidery floss

Thin pink ribbon

Printed label (optional)

Wavy ruler (optional)

WHAT YOU DO

1 Use the templates to cut two ornament shapes from the green felt, one slightly smaller ornament shape from the batting, four flower shapes from pink, and two ornament topper shapes from the light green, cutting along the bottom with pinking shears, as indicated.

2 With the ¼-inch (6 mm) hole punch, cut 14 holes from light green felt, snipping off any fuzz not cut by the punch.

Tip: Before using the hole punch, first stiffen the felt with an iron and spray sizing or light starch.

3 Sew the light green ornament topper to the ornament front by creating straight stitches that correspond with the zigzag you cut with the pinking shears. Repeat this process for the ornament back.

4 If you're using your ornament as a gift tag, attach the printed label to the ornament back.

5 Draw a line for the dots across the center of the ornament front, using a wavy ruler or the photo as a guide. Attach the 10 light green dots (with a bead on top of each) along this line with single stitches.

6 Baste the flowers in place on the ornament. Sew each petal down with a straight stitch and a beaded stitch. Sew the remaining light green dots in the flower center with a single beaded stitch. Trim the two flowers that extend past the ornament edge.

7 Place the ornament batting shape between the ornament front and back, and baste the layers together. Sew a green blanket stitch around the edge of the ornament.

8 Using the smaller hole punch, punch a hole through the ornament topper, and feed the hanging ribbon through.

Wood clothespins add a homey touch—
and a practical element—to these simple
Perching Dove ornaments.

Perching Doves

DESIGNER: AMANDA CARESTIO

WHAT YOU NEED

(to make one)

Basic sewing kit (page 9)

Template (page 116)

Cream felt, two 5 x 3-inch (12.7 x 7.6 cm) squares

Blue embroidery floss

2 buttons, $\frac{1}{8}$-inch (3 mm) diameter (for eyes)

Stuffing

Clothespin

WHAT YOU DO

1 Cut two dove shapes from cream felt using the template.

2 Using two strands of the blue embroidery floss, stitch the wing shape on the ornament front and back with backstitches. Stitch the button eyes in place with floss, making sure they match up on the front and back.

3 Starting under the wing at the bottom of the dove, begin blanket-stitching around the outside edge.

4 Stop about 1$\frac{1}{2}$ inches (3.8 cm) before the starting point and stuff the dove, filling it quite full so it has some dimension.

5 Stitch the dove closed and tie off, but do not cut the excess floss.

6 Position the dove on top of the clothespin, and then use the excess floss to attach it to the clothespin. Run the thread through the clothespin spring and through the bottom of the dove, catching a little of the side of the dove and pulling tight so it's secure.

Ornaments •

25

This sweet
Gingerbread House
won't get stale anytime soon.

Gingerbread House

DESIGNER: LAURA HOWARD

WHAT YOU DO

1 Use the templates to cut two house shapes from light brown felt, one roof shape from white felt, and one door shape from white felt.

2 Position the white roof piece on the front house shape, and stitch it in place along the scalloped bottom edge only. Use white thread and one small vertical stitch between each scallop.

3 Cut an assortment of tiny felt circles from the felt scraps, and sew them onto the roof at random. Use one small stitch of matching thread to attach each circle, sewing through both the white and the light brown felt.

4 Position the door on the bottom left of the house, and pin it in place.

5 Sew around the edge of the door using red thread and backstitch to form a continuous decorative line of stitches. Then sew a small cross shape in the center of the door, and make small angled stitches to form a circular window shape.

6 Using a double thickness of white thread, neatly backstitch a window frame shape next to the door. Begin by stitching a cross shape to get the window the size you want, and then stitch around the edges to complete the frame.

7 Fold the length of ribbon in half. Turn the house front over, and position the looped ribbon so it emerges from the top of the roof. Sew the cut ends onto the light brown felt. If the ribbon has a pattern, take care that it will show at the front of the ornament.

8 Place the two house shapes together with wrong sides facing. Using white thread, start at one bottom corner and stitch up the side, around the roof, and down the other side of the house, leaving a hole for stuffing.

9 Fill the house loosely with stuffing or small scraps of felt or fabric. Sew across the bottom of the ornament to finish.

WHAT YOU NEED

Basic sewing kit (page 9)

Templates (page 121)

Light brown felt

White felt

Red, orange, yellow, and green felt scraps

White, red, and various thread to match scraps

Narrow red ribbon, 6 inches (15.2 cm)

Stuffing or felt scraps

These little **Holiday Toadstools** are hand stitched,
making them the perfect take-along project.

Holiday Toadstools

DESIGNER: CATHY GAUBERT

WHAT YOU NEED

(to make one)

Basic sewing kit (page 9)

Templates (page 122)

White or cream wool felt, 4 x 4 inches (10.2 x 10.2 cm)

Red wool felt, 4 x 4 inches (10.2 x 10.2 cm)

White heavyweight thread

Red thread

White and black embroidery floss

Stuffing

Long darning needle

Baker's twine, 8 inches (20.3 cm)

WHAT YOU DO

1 Use the templates to cut one stem shape, one face shape, and five dots from white felt. Cut one cap shape from the red felt.

2 To make the stem, roll the rectangle up widthwise so that you have a stem that is 2 inches (5 cm) tall. Whipstitch the edge to the roll with the heavyweight thread.

3 With right sides facing up, match up the curve on the cap piece to the curve on the top of the face piece. Slightly overlap the pieces (with the red on top), and stitch them together with red thread.

4 Sew a running stitch along the outer edge of the felt circle using a doubled length (about 20 inches [50.8 cm]) of heavyweight thread. Pull the thread to gather the circle, and then begin stuffing the cap. Continue pulling the gathers tighter and adding more stuffing. You may need to make a few stitches here and there as you tighten up the opening, but make sure to leave a space for the stem. Do not cut your thread; you'll use it to attach the stem.

5 With the stem's seam to the back, place the stem into the cap opening. It should fit rather snugly. Attach the top front of the stem to the redcap right under the chin.

Continue stitching along under the redcap, attaching the cap to the stem.

6 Refer to the photo of the finished redcaps for eye and mouth placement, or design your own face. Mark the placement with straight pins, and use two strands of black embroidery floss to stitch French knots for the eyes and one or two small stitches for the mouth.

7 Use straight pins to pin the dots onto the redcap. With white floss, attach each dot with a single stitch.

8 With the large darning needle, stitch through the top of the redcap with the baker's twine. Pull the ends of the twine up, and knot the tails to create a hanger.

Relive your childhood with this holiday tribute to a classic snack, Animal Crackers with sprinkles.

Animal Crackers

DESIGNER: SUZIE MILLIONS

WHAT YOU NEED

Basic sewing kit (page 9)

Templates (page 124)

White and pink felt, 9 x 12-inch (22.9 x 30.5 cm) sheet each

Seed beads in an assortment of colors

Gold cord, 24 inches (61 cm)

White and pink embroidery floss

Stuffing

Blunt tool

Glue

White and pink feathers

WHAT YOU DO

1 Fold each sheet of felt in half. Using the templates, cut two animals from pink and two from white so you have an ornament front and back for each animal.

2 Sew the seed beads to outside of each felt panel with one continuous thread, zigzagging to avoid long stitches.

3 Cut a 6-inch (15.2 cm) length of gold cord for each ornament. For each length, double the cord to make a loop, and tie a knot near the base.

4 Cut a long length of embroidery floss, matching up contrasting colors (white and pink) of felt and floss. Position the gold cord roughly in the center of the animal's back, with the knot about 1/2 inch (1.3 cm) below the edge of the panel. Tack the gold cord to the felt panel by stitching over it a couple of times, being careful not to stitch all the way through the felt.

5 Position the second panel on the first, with the beaded sides out. Blanket-stitch all the way around the edges, stopping about an inch (2.5 cm) before you meet the point where you began.

6 Stuff the ornament until it's plump, and use a blunt tool—such as a skewer—to push the stuffing into legs and other details.

7 Finish the blanket-stitching, and make your final stitches directly through the gold cord. Knot the thread, and use your blunt tool to poke the thread tail into the ornament.

8 Press the end of the tool gently between the stitches to create a guide hole on top of the animal's head. Put a small dot of glue on the outside of the hole, and gently slip the feather in.

Who says Christmas trees can't bear a cute *Apple & Pear*?

Apple & Pear

DESIGNER: CONSTANÇA CABRAL

WHAT YOU NEED

Basic sewing kit (page 9)

Templates (page121)

Red felt, 12 x 12 inches (30.5 x 30.5 cm)

Light blue felt, 11 x 14 inches (27.9 x 35.6 cm)

2 lengths of baker's twine (or ribbon or rick-rack), each 8 inches (20.3 cm)

Red, light blue, and white thread

Stuffing

White, dark red, and turquoise felt scraps (for leaves)

1 white button

1 red button

WHAT YOU DO

1 Using the templates, cut two apple shapes from red felt and two pear shapes from light blue felt.

Tip: Cut through two layers of felt at once to get two matching shapes for the front and back of each ornament.

2 Fold each length of the twine, ribbon, or rickrack in half to make a loop, and tie a knot in the ends. Place each loop between the ornament front and back, at the center top of each ornament. Pin the loops in position.

3 Sew the apple front and back together using a sewing machine or by hand, starting at the bottom of the apple and using the red thread. Be sure to leave a generous distance between your stitches and the edge of the apple. You'll pink these edges in the final steps. Sew around the edge, catching the loop and leaving a 1½-inch (3.8 cm) hole for stuffing. Repeat with the pear shapes using the light blue thread.

4 Fill the apple and the pear using small pieces of stuffing.

5 Sew the openings closed, backstitching at each end.

6 Using pinking or scallop shears, trim the edges of each ornament. Be careful not to cut the loops.

7 Using the leaf templates, cut one small and one large leaf for each fruit. Arrange them nicely on top of the fruit, over the base of the loop, and sew one stitch to keep them in place. Use the red thread to sew the white button on top of the apple's leaves. Use the white thread to sew the red button on top of the pear's leaves.

These **Three Wise Fish** are happier on your Christmas tree than in a fishbowl.

Three Wise Fish

DESIGNER: LISA JORDAN

WHAT YOU NEED

Basic sewing kit (page 9)

Templates (page 124)

Felted orange wool sweater, commercial felt, or eco felt, one 4-inch (10.2 cm) square and one 1 1/2-inch (3.8 cm) square

Embroidery floss

2 buttons (preferably shank or 2-holed)

Jute, hemp twine, or narrow ribbon

Stuffing

WHAT YOU DO

1 Cut two body shapes and two fins for each fish ornament, arranging the templates on the felt squares so you're able to make good use of the space.

2 With two strands of embroidery floss, add some decorative stitches to one side of the body to suggest scales and a tail fin.

3 Place a fin piece on the body of your fish, and stitch it on using a few decorative stitches. Sew on the button eye.

4 Repeat the previous two steps for the other side of the fish, arranging the fin and eye so they match up neatly when the two pieces are sewn together.

5 Match the front and back pieces up with wrong sides facing, and begin stitching the two pieces together at the bottom center using a blanket stitch. Continue stitching until you reach the center top of the back or until the fish hangs level when dangled from the embroidery floss.

6 Make a short loop with your hemp, twine, or ribbon, and knot the end. Insert the knot into the interior of the ornament, just beneath the stitching, and continue stitching around and over the hanging loop. The knot will be trapped under the stitching.

7 Continue sewing around the fish until a 1-inch (2.5 cm) opening remains, and then stuff the ornament.

8 Finish sewing the fish, concealing the bottom knot inside the stitching.

When it's time to pack up the holiday decorations, these
Sew Merry pincushions can go in your sewing basket.

Sew Merry

DESIGNER: CINDY GREY

WHAT YOU NEED

(to make the brown pincushion)

Basic sewing kit (page 9)

Templates (page 124)

Light brown felt

White baby rickrack

White embroidery floss

Bottle cap, 1-inch (2.5 cm) size

Strong sewing thread

Stuffing

Narrow white ribbon, 10 inches (25.4 cm)

Decorative pin

WHAT YOU DO

1 From the light brown felt, cut one 1 x 4¹/₄-inch (2.5 x 10.8 cm) strip, one 1¹/₄-inch (3.2 cm) square, and one 3-inch (7.6 cm) square.

2 Center two pieces of baby rickrack onto the center of the strip, extending the ends of the rickrack past one edge of the strip. Using one strand of white embroidery floss, sew the rickrack onto the strip, but do not tack it down all the way to the edge of the felt.

3 Using two strands of white floss, create French knots between the two strips of rickrack and along the top and bottom edges of the rickrack, stopping before you get to the edge.

4 Wrap the embroidered strip around the bottle cap. Using the strong sewing thread, baste the two edges of the embroidered strip together, overlapping slightly so it will be a tight fit around the bottle cap.

5 Overlap the loose rickrack ends so they line up with the rickrack on the other side.

Make the remainder of French knots on the top, bottom, and center of rickrack, being sure to sew through both layers of felt.

6 To make the bottom of the pincushion, cut off the corners of the 1¹/₄-inch (3.2 cm) light brown square to create a rough circle. Put the bottle cap back inside the basted strip, and fit the round piece on top of the bottle cap. *continued*

7 With a 40-inch (101.6 cm) length of white floss, blanket-stitch around the edge, attaching the side strip to the bottom circle. When you get all the way around, pull the threaded needle to the inside of the strip; you'll use the same thread to attach the top of the pincushion.

8 To make the pincushion top, round off the corners of the 3-inch (7.6 cm) square so it becomes a rough circle. Using strong thread or six strands of embroidery floss, knot one end and baste around the outer edge to create a drawstring. Stuff the pouch, and tighten the basting thread. Tie off and cut the basting thread. Stuff the top into the bottle cap, keeping it as smooth as possible.

9 Insert the top and cap back into the bottom strip. Arrange the outer strip so that it fits snugly around the top. Using the thread that is still on the inside of the strip, blanket-stitch around the top to attach the side strip to the top of the pincushion.

10 With the thin white ribbon, make a loop for hanging. Use a decorative pin to secure the ribbon loop in the center of the pincushion.

11 Follow the same basic steps and the stitching templates on page 124 to create the other pincushions.

Beaded Tassel Drops

DESIGNER: CATHY ZIEGELE

As lovely as any made from glass, these Beaded Tassel Drops only look fragile.

Beaded Tassel Drops

WHAT YOU NEED

(to make the blue-green ornament)

Basic sewing kit (page 9)

Templates (page 122)

Light blue and blue-green felt

Fabric pen

Blue, yellow-green, yellow, and blue-green embroidery floss

Double-sided tape (optional)

Blue glass 6/0 beads

Stuffing

Two ¼-inch (6 mm) jump rings

WHAT YOU DO

1 Using the templates, cut three large ovals from blue-green felt and three small ovals from light blue felt.

2 With a fabric pen, mark a stitching line around the interior of one large oval shape, ¼ inch (6 mm) in from the outside edge. Sew a double-threaded running stitch (page 10) along this line using blue floss for the running stitch, yellow-green floss for one side of the threading, and yellow floss for the other. The space between your running stitches will determine the size of the chain it creates, so try to space them evenly. Repeat this process with the other two large oval shapes.

3 Center the small oval on the large oval, and hold it in place with basting or double-sided tape. Sew a double-threaded running stitch ⅛ inch (3 mm) in from the edge using yellow-green for the running stitch and blue for both sides of the threading. Sew a yellow French knot inside each of the blue ovals. Repeat this process with the other two large oval shapes.

4 With wrong sides together, sew a blanket stitch down each side to join the large ovals, picking up a bead before you complete each stitch. When you're stitching the last side, stop two-thirds of the way down, stuff the ornament, and resume sewing it closed.

5 Sew a jump ring at each end of the ornament.

6 Pull out about 2 yards (1.8 m) of blue-green embroidery thread, leaving it attached to the skein for weight. Thread this length onto a large needle, and feed it through one jump ring. Using your thumb and forefinger, wrap the thread around your thumb and the jump ring, feeding it through the jump ring each time. When your tassel is fat enough, wrap the needle and thread around it $^{1}/_{2}$ inch (1.3 cm) below the jump ring. Wrap the thread a few more times to make a band; then sew through the band and tie off. Cut the tassel open, and trim it evenly.

7 Knot a loop of floss onto the other jump ring to create a hanger.

Give a set of these vintage-inspired,
Merry Little Ornaments as a present,
or use them individually as gift tags.

Merry Little Ornaments

DESIGNER: CATHY ZIEGELE

WHAT YOU NEED

(to make the pink ornament)

Basic sewing kit (page 9)

Templates (page 122)

Pink and red felt

Thin cotton batting

Printed fabric label (optional)

Fabric pen

Red and white seed beads

Pink and red embroidery floss

Hole punch

Narrow red ribbon

WHAT YOU DO

1 Using the templates, cut two ornament shapes from pink felt, one slightly smaller ornament shape from the batting, and two flower shapes from the red felt.

2 If you plan to use the ornament as a gift tag, stitch the painted fabric label onto the ornament back (see page 23).

3 With a fabric pen, draw two sets of parallel lines $1/4$ inch (6 mm) apart across the ornament front at an angle, leaving $1^3/8$ inches (3.5 cm) between the two sets of lines for the flowers.

4 Along each line, use red floss to stitch a repeating pattern of one running stitch, one red bead, one running stitch, etc.

5 Using the photo as a guide, tack the flowers in place. Stitch down the centerline of each petal using three white beads and red thread.

6 Sew six red beads in the center of each flower, starting with one in the center and adding five around it.

Tip: If you'd like to add an ornament topper, use the template to cut one out, and stitch it to the top of the ornament front.

7 Stack the batting ornament shape in between the front and back of your ornament, and baste it all together. Sew a blanket stitch in pink floss around the entire ornament shape.

8 Punch a hole $1/8$ inch (3 mm) in from the stitching at the top of the ornament for the hanging ribbon. Feed the ribbon through the hole, and knot it.

These felt *Golden Partridges* with glittering bead eyes would be welcome in any pear (or Christmas) tree.

Golden Partridges

DESIGNER: KAREN DE NARDI

WHAT YOU NEED

Basic sewing kit (page 9)

Templates (page 124)

Yellow-brown felt

Scraps of patterned fabric

Cream embroidery floss

Crystal beads

Stuffing

Thin cream ribbon, 9 1/2 inches (24.1 cm)

WHAT YOU DO

1 Using the template, cut out two bird shapes from the yellow-brown felt.

2 Cut a small piece of patterned fabric using the wing template. Carefully make small snips into the fabric edges. Using your fingernails or a cool iron, press these edges towards the wrong side of the fabric, and tuck them under to prevent the fabric from fraying.

3 Using three strands of the cream embroidery floss, stitch the wing onto one of the bird pieces, checking that all of the edges are tucked under as you make your way around.

4 Make an eye for the bird by sewing on the bead. Add a wing and a bead eye to the ornament back.

5 Stack the bird front on top of the bird back with wrong sides together. Starting in the middle of the bird's back, begin to blanket-stitch around the bird shape to join the two body pieces together.

6 Before you get back to your starting point, stuff the bird as firmly as desired and complete the edge stitching. Leave the thread hanging.

7 Attach the ribbon to the back of the bird using the remaining thread.

Share the love this Christmas with these fabric and felt *Holiday Hearts.*

Holiday Hearts

DESIGNER: CONSTANÇA CABRAL

WHAT YOU NEED

(to make one)

Basic sewing kit (page 9)

Templates (page 121)

Red or turquoise felt, 12 x 12 inches (30.5 x 30.5 cm)

Fabric scraps in matching and contrasting colors

Matching and contrasting thread colors (we've used white and red)

Buttons in contrasting colors

String, ribbon, rickrack, or baker's twine, 8 inches (20.3 cm)

Stuffing

WHAT YOU DO

1 Using the templates, cut out the two large heart shapes from the red felt.

2 Decorate the front of the heart. You can attach a smaller fabric heart shape (with the template provided), sew on a small square of fabric and buttons, or cover the entire heart shape with buttons. (Use pinking shears or scallop shears to cut the decorative fabric.)

3 Make a hanging loop with the length of string, ribbon, rickrack , or

twine, and tie a knot at its end. Place the loop between the front and the back felt shapes, at the center top of the heart. Pin in place.

4 Sew the heart shapes together using your sewing machine or by hand, with wrong sides together and starting on the bottom of the ornament. Be sure to leave a good amount of space between your seam and the edge of the ornament; you'll be pinking this edge in a later step. Sew all around the shape, catching the loop and leaving a 1¹/₂-inch (3.8 cm) hole for stuffing.

Tip: Experiment with matching and contrasting thread colors to achieve the look that pleases you.

5 Fill the heart with stuffing, and sew the opening closed, backstitching at each end.

6 Using pinking shears or scallop shears, trim the edges of the ornament. Sew a button at the base of the loop.

Simple stitched details
and button eyes add
character to these sweet little
Holiday Hoot owls.

Holiday Hoot

DESIGNER: LISA JORDAN

WHAT YOU NEED

(to make one)

Basic sewing kit (page 9)

Templates (page 122)

Brown felt (or felted sweater), two 3 x 3½-inch (7.6 x 8.9 cm) pieces and one 1-inch (2.5 cm) square (for the eyelids; optional)

Cream felt, 2 x 2 inches (5 x 5 cm) (for the belly and face)

Yellow felt, 1 x 2 inches (2.5 x 5 cm)

Scrap of orange felt

Fabric glue

Orange, brown, yellow, and cream embroidery floss

Two ½-inch (1.3 cm) buttons (preferably shank or 2-hole)

Jute, hemp twine, or narrow ribbon (for the hanging loop)

Stuffing

WHAT YOU DO

1 From the templates, cut two body shapes from the brown felt, one face and one belly shape from cream, two eye shapes from yellow, and one beak shape from the orange. If you choose, cut small half circles from brown to create eyelids.

2 Arrange the belly, face, and eye felt pieces where you'd like them on the front body piece. Tack the pieces down with a dot of fabric glue to keep them in place while you sew.

3 Divide a length of cream embroidery floss into a three-strand piece, and whipstitch the belly onto the body. Using a three-strand piece of brown floss, add a few decorative stitches to the belly to suggest feathers.

4 Stitch the cream face shape in place using a whipstitch or a running stitch. Stitch the yellow eyes to the face shape using a three-strand piece of yellow floss.

5 Place the button eyes on top of the yellow eye pieces, and stitch them down securely. If you've chosen to give your owl eyelids, attach them now, partially covering the button eyes.

6 Embroider or stitch the beak to the face using the orange floss.

7 Place the ornament front on top of the back piece with wrong sides facing and matching the edges. Begin stitching the two pieces together at the bottom center, using a blanket stitch and brown floss. Continue stitching until you reach the center top of the head.

8 Make a short loop—3 to 4 inches (7.6 to 10.2 cm) works well—with your hemp, twine, or ribbon, and knot the end. Insert the knot into the interior of the ornament, just beneath the stitches, and continue stitching over the hanging loop. The knot will be secured under the stitching.

Tip: If you're using narrow ribbon for the hanging loop, be sure to make a large enough knot so it doesn't slip through the stitch.

9 Continue sewing around the owl until about 1 inch (2.5 cm) remains. Then stuff the ornament. Finish stitching the owl, tie a knot, and hide it to finish.

Raid your button stash to embellish
these sweet felt *Silver Bells*.

Silver Bells

DESIGNER: AMANDA CARESTIO

DESIGNER: AMANDA CARESTIO

WHAT YOU NEED

(to make one)

Basic sewing kit (page 9)

Templates (page 116)

Cream felt, two 5-inch (12.7 cm) squares

Scraps of felt for accent color

Embroidery floss, tan and accent color

7 to 10 buttons in accent color

Cream sewing thread

Stuffing

Jute

WHAT YOU DO

1 Using the templates, cut two bell shapes from cream felt and one strip from the accent color. Also cut a 1¹/₄-inch-diameter (3.2 cm) circle from the accent color.

2 Pin the strip to the bell front, and blanket-stitch it in place along the top and bottom edge with the embroidery floss that matches your accent color. Fold the small felt circle in half, and stitch it to itself along the curved edge using the same accent color floss.

3 Stitch your buttons in place on the strip with the sewing thread.

4 Pin the bell front and back together with wrong sides facing. Starting at the top center, blanket-stitch around the outside edge with tan floss. Stop when you reach the bottom edge of the bell.

5 Sandwich the half circle between the layers at the bottom center of the bell. Continue blanket-stitching over the half circle. This stitching will attach the half circle to the ornament front. Pull the thread back through the ornament and blanket-stitch along the back side, this time attaching the half circle to the ornament back.

6 Continue stitching around the bell, stopping about 1¹/₂ inches (3.8 cm) before you get to your starting point. Stuff the bell.

7 Cut and fold an 8-inch (20.3 cm) length of jute in half. Knot one end of the loop and insert the knot at the top of the ornament. Continue stitching to close the bell, stitching over the knot to secure it.

8 Sew a single button in place at the top of the bell, stitching through the hanging loop knot to further secure it.

Bright rainbow circles of craft felt are built up to create a 3D effect in these modern **Layer Play** baubles.

Layer Play

DESIGNER: LAURA HOWARD

WHAT YOU NEED

Basic sewing kit (page 9)

Template (page 122)

Assorted felt scraps

Black felt

Black sewing thread

Narrow black ribbon

WHAT YOU DO

1 Cut out a small felt circle using the template. This will become the top circle on your bauble.

2 Place the small circle on top of a second felt scrap and cut around it, leaving a narrow border around the small circle.

3 Repeat this process to make another larger circle, and continue until you've cut seven circles in different sizes and colors. Use black felt for the final (largest) circle.

4 Use all the circles as templates to cut out seven matching circles, so you end up with seven pairs.

5 Cut seven pairs of circles for each bauble you want to make, using the pieces you've already cut as your templates. You can make each bauble in the set identical or alternate the colors to make each one slightly different. In each set, the largest circles should always be black felt.

6 Layer the circles to make two matching piles per ornament. Using black thread, sew eight large stitches through the center of each pile to hold all the circles together, forming a decorative star shape in the center of the bauble.

7 Cut a 6-inch (15.2 cm) length of narrow black ribbon. Loop the ribbon, and sew the cut ends to the back of one of the black circles.

8 Hold two matching sets of circles together back to back, and sew the black outer circles together using black thread. Repeat for each bauble.

Ornaments • 53

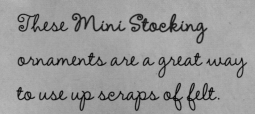

These Mini Stocking ornaments are a great way to use up scraps of felt.

Mini Stockings

DESIGNER: CATHY ZIEGELE

WHAT YOU NEED

Basic sewing kit (page 9)

Templates (page 123)

Assorted felt sheets and scraps

Assorted shape punches and wavy rulers

Fabric pen

Various colors of embroidery floss

Hole punch

Narrow black ribbon

WHAT YOU DO

1 Cut six mini stocking shapes using the template, three in black (for the backs) and three in various colors. Cut one heel and toe for each stocking from contrasting colored felt.

2 Cut out your various design elements. Use a wavy ruler and a fabric pen to draw and cut out some felt strips for the top border pieces. Cut strips of felt into diamond shapes or tiny squares to make a checkerboard. Cut out a variety of leaf and flower shapes.

3 Position your elements onto each stocking front. Sew the elements down with various embroidery stitches: lazy daisy, running stitch, backstitch, double-threaded running stitch (page 10), and French knots.

4 Sew a running stitch from each toe to heel piece in a contrasting color of floss.

5 Position the ornament front on top of the black back piece. Blanket-stitch the front to the back with black floss leaving the top open.

6 Punch a hole near the top for your ribbon hanger. Feed the ribbon through the hole, and loop it back over itself.

Variation idea:

Use the same basic steps and the template on page 123 to make mini stocking ornaments with curly toes.

Classic but with a touch of mod style, these sassy little Christmas Tree ornaments are a cinch to make.

Oh, Christmas Trees

DESIGNER: ULA PHELEP

WHAT YOU NEED

Basic sewing kit (page 9)

Template (page 117)

Pink and green felt

Pink and green embroidery floss

Thin green ribbon

Double-sided tape

WHAT YOU DO

1 Using the template, cut two tree shapes, one from green felt and one from pink.

2 With a pencil, draw swirls onto the green tree shape. Thread your needle with pink embroidery thread, and stitch through the lines with a simple backstitch on the right side of the shape.

3 Attach two ends of the ribbon onto the middle of the pink tree shape using double-sided tape. Stack the green tree on top of the pink tree with wrong sides together, sandwiching the ribbon in between the layers.

4 Using green floss and a whipstitch along the outside edge, stitch the two tree shapes together.

A felt version of a traditional paper decoration, these *Retro Strip Ornaments* come together with just a stitch or two.

Retro Strip Ornaments

DESIGNER: AMANDA CARESTIO

WHAT YOU NEED

Basic sewing kit (page 9)

Purple and hot pink felt, $\frac{1}{4}$ yard (.2 m) or
9 x 12-inch (22.9 x 30.5 cm) sheet each

Gold embroidery floss

Gold cord

WHAT YOU DO

1 Cut $1\frac{1}{4}$-inch-wide (3.2 cm) strips from the felt. From the purple felt, cut a strip that is 17 inches (43.2 cm) long and one that is $11\frac{1}{2}$ inches (29.2 cm) long. From the hot pink felt, cut a strip that is $14\frac{1}{2}$ inches (36.8 cm) long and one that is 5 inches (12.7 cm) long.

Tip: If you're using sheets of felt, cut two $8\frac{1}{2}$-inch (21.6 cm) strips and two $6\frac{3}{4}$-inch (17.1 cm) strips from purple as well as two $7\frac{1}{4}$-inch (18.4 cm) strips and one 5-inch (12.7 cm) strip from hot pink.

2 Fold all the strips, except the 5-inch (12.7 cm) one, in half and sandwich them one inside the other, lining up the top edges and placing the short hot pink strip in the middle. With three strands of the gold embroidery floss, stitch (okay, it's *almost* no sew) the layers together at the fold, hiding the starting and finishing knots in between the layers.

3 Line up the bottoms of the loops, sandwiching the end of the 5-inch (12.7 cm) strip between them. With gold floss, stitch the layers together, again hiding the knots.

4 Thread a 5-inch (12.7 cm) length of gold cord under the stitching at the top of the ornament, and knot the ends together.

Quick, make a wish on a **Star Bright** that's spangled with a sequin and lines of sparkling bugle beads.

Star Bright

DESIGNER: LAURA HOWARD

WHAT YOU NEED

Basic sewing kit (page 9)

Templates (page 122)

Felt scraps in white and assorted shades of blue

White and dark blue thread

Large star sequin

Blue bugle beads

Thin blue ribbon, 5 inches (12.7 cm)

WHAT YOU DO

1 Cut out all five pattern shapes using the templates provided. Cut the smallest star and tail pieces from white felt and cut the other pieces from assorted shades of blue.

2 Layer the tail shapes and star shapes so you have two stacks of felt pieces in graduating sizes.

3 Place the stack of tail shapes on a piece of dark blue felt, leaving room to add the star shapes later. Appliqué the tail shapes, using neat stitches and white thread. You only need to sew around the smaller shape, as this will hold both pieces in place.

4 Position the stack of star shapes overlapping the tail, so the tail shoots from the star at an angle.

5 Appliqué the star shapes with white stitches. Then use matching thread to stitch the largest star to the dark blue felt, sewing flush with the medium star to keep your stitches hidden.

6 Sew a large star sequin in the center of the felt star pieces, using thread that matches the sequin.

7 Sew bugle beads in four lines along the tail. Start each line of beads at the star and work towards the other end of the tail.

8 Cut through the bottom dark blue felt layer following the shape of the star and tail, leaving a narrow border of felt around each edge. Then use this cut shape as a template to cut a matching piece of dark blue felt for the back of the ornament.

9 Fold the length of ribbon in half, and sew the cut ends to the back of the ornament front, so the star hangs at an angle.

10 Sew the ornament front and back together, stitching around the border of dark blue felt using matching thread.

Tiny embroidery hoops frame this
Sweet Trio of yummy little ornaments.

Sweet Trio

DESIGNER: CATHY GAUBERT

WHAT YOU NEED

Basic sewing kit (page 9)

Templates (page 117)

Gray wool felt, three 4-inch (10.2 cm) squares

Black felt, three 4-inch (10.2 cm) squares

Brown wool felt, 3-inch (7.6 cm) square

Scraps of red, aqua, green, yellow, and white wool felt

Three 3-inch (7.6 cm) embroidery hoops

Red, white, and black embroidery floss

Fabric glue

WHAT YOU DO

1 Using the templates, cut out three gray background shapes, three black back cover shapes, one white candy cane shape, one brown gingerbread couple, and four gumdrop shapes in assorted colors.

2 Stretch each gray felt shape onto an embroidery hoop.

3 Using the photo as a guide, position the candy cane shape in the center of one hoop. With two strands of red embroidery floss, make 15 to 17 long stitches over the candy cane to hold it in place.

4 Position the gumdrops on the second hoop. Using two strands of white floss, make tiny random stitches all over the gumdrops to attach them to the gray felt.

5 Position the gingerbread couple in the center of the third hoop. Stitch black French knots for the eyes and white French knots for the mouths. The fellow has three red French knots down his front, while the gal has a heart made with two small diagonal stitches. The icing detail on the arms, legs, and the skirt are made with white floss in the same manner as the candy cane stripes. For all of these details, use two strands of floss.

6 To make the back sides nice and neat, cut away the excess gray felt from the back, flush with the hoop. Glue the black felt covers to the back, trimming if necessary.

7 With red floss, tie a hanging loop to the screw on each hoop.

Fa la la la decorations

The tree isn't the only place to show your holiday cheer. Bring a bit of comfort and joy to your holiday table, your mantle, the front door, a snowy windowsill, the banister, and even the bedroom. These homey felt decorations have a natural charm that warms the heart and cheers the spirit.

*Use the animal templates provided or cut silhouettes of your own favorite creatures to make a felt winter wonderland full of **Christmas Pines**.*

Christmas Pines

DESIGNER: CATHY GAUBERT

WHAT YOU NEED

(To make one tree)

Basic sewing kit (page 9)

Templates (page 125)

Green wool felt, 6 x 10 inches (15.2 x 25.4 cm)

Red wool felt, 1 inch (2.5 cm) square

White wool felt, 2 inches (5 cm) square

Water-soluble pen (optional)

Red wool yarn

Yarn needle (with a sharp point and large eye)

White and red embroidery floss

Green thread

Blunt tool (for turning)

Wool or polyester stuffing

WHAT YOU DO

1 Using the tree template as a pattern to cut or trace around, cut one tree from the green felt. Use the rotary cutter with a scallop blade (or the pinking shears) along the bottom of the tree and around the base piece. Cut two redcap shapes from the red felt, and two stems and one animal shape from the white felt.

Tip: If you're using a rotary cutter, you may have to flip the blade over so that when you cut out the base of the tree, you get a scalloped edge on *it* instead of the piece you're cutting from.

2 With a water-soluble pen, mark the placement of the red berries on the tree. With a length of red wool yarn and the yarn needle, make a French knot at each mark.

Tip: When making individual French knots, leave a 3 1/2-inch (8.9 cm) tail at the back, make the French knot, go back through the fabric, and then knot the tails together.

3 Cut a 20-inch (50.8 cm) piece of white floss, and separate it into two-strand sections. Referring to the photo and using small stitches, attach the squirrel and the stems of the redcap to the tree. Use red floss to attach the top of the redcaps to the tree, and then create little spots with white French knots.

4 Fold the tree in half with right sides together, and using a 1/8-inch (.3 cm) seam allowance, stitch from top to bottom with green thread. Turn right side out, using a blunt tool to gently poke out the top of the tree. Stuff firmly, stopping about 1/2 inch (1.3 cm) from the bottom edge.

5 Whipstitch the base to the bottom edge of the tree. Continue to add a bit of stuffing as you are stitching the opening closed so that the tree is stuffed firmly all the way down to the base.

6 Follow these same steps to create the other trees in your forest.

You're going to smile every December when you open the box where you've tucked Gingerman and his Sugar Friend away for safekeeping.

Gingerman & Sugar Friend

DESIGNER: CATHY GAUBERT

(To make the Gingerman)

Basic sewing kit (page 9)

Templates (page 117)

Brown felted wool (or felt), 6 x 6 inches (15.2 x 15.2 cm)

Brown wool felt, 3 x 3 inches (7.6 x 7.6 cm)

Cream wool felt, 3 x 3 inches (7.6 x 7.6 cm)

Red wool felt, 6 x 4 inches (15.2 x 10.2 cm)

Brown, red, and white thread

Black, white, red, and brown embroidery floss

Wool or polyester stuffing

Small jingle bell

WHAT YOU DO

1 Using the template, cut out two bodies from the felted wool. (See page 8 for information on creating felted wool.)

2 Trace the two arms onto doubled brown wool felt. With brown thread, stitch around the arm shape, working ⅛ inch (3 mm) inside the traced line for both arms. Cut the arms out on the line.

3 Do the same for the legs with cream felt, but use the white thread. Cut out the legs just as you did the arms. Using the photo as a guide, machine-stitch back and forth across the legs with red thread to create four stripes.

4 With right sides facing out, stitch the body together around the outside edge, leaving the bottom open. Stuff firmly, stopping about ½ inch (1.3 cm) from the bottom opening.

Tip: If you want, stitch the face details before you sew the front and back body pieces together.

continued

These two simple-to-stitch characters are happy to sit around on a windowsill or tabletop. They look as if they might have found the eggnog, don't they?

5 Place the top edge of each leg into the bottom opening, and stitch across the bottom once or twice, being sure to catch the legs in the seam.

6 Cut two pieces of brown embroidery floss to attach the arms to the body. If you like, stitch a decorative "X" to attach the arms.

7 Using a full strand of the white embroidery floss (about 24 inches [61 cm] long), embroider the mouth by making French knots, referring to the template for placement. With black floss, make French knots for the eyes.

Tip: To hide your starting and ending knots, go in from the top of the head; the pointy party hat will cover this area later.

8 To create the hat, trace the pattern onto a doubled layer of red felt (with right sides facing out), stitch just inside of your traced line on the left and right edge, and cut out along the line. Place the hat onto the head, and hand-stitch it in place, adding stuffing as you work. With red embroidery floss, attach a tiny jingle bell to the top point of the hat.

9 Use the button template to cut three circles from the red felt scraps left over from the hat. With white embroidery floss, attach each button to the front of the body.

10 To create the sugar friend version, use cream felt and thread.

The trapunto leaves on this Boughs and Berries wreath only look fancy. Stuffing the shapes from behind is an easy way to make foliage that won't wither.

Boughs & Berries

DESIGNER: AMANDA CARESTIO

WHAT YOU NEED

Basic sewing kit (page 9)

Template (page 117)

Blue felt, ½ yard (.5 m)

Dark green felt, ¼ yard (.2 m)

Scraps of white felt

Dark green, blue, and white thread

6 small red buttons, less than ¾ inch (1.9 cm) in diameter

Stuffing

Chopstick or knitting needle

Tip: To cut two shapes at the same time, simply double over the felt and cut through two layers at once.

WHAT YOU DO

1 Cut two 15½-inch (39.4 cm) circles from the blue felt with pinking shears. Draw a 6½-inch (16.5 cm) circle in the center of each large circle shape, and use pinking shears to cut out the inner circle.

2 Cut two strips of dark green felt with shears: one that is 2 x 25 inches (5 x 63.5 cm) and one that is 2 x 50 inches (5 x 127 cm).

3 Using the template, cut out 24 leaf shapes from the dark green felt. Arrange the leaves on the right side of the front wreath shape, following the project photo as a guide. Pin the leaves in place and stitch around the outside of each leaf with white thread.

4 Cut six ¾-inch (1.9 cm) circles from the white felt, and then pin and stitch them in place with dark green thread. Stitch a red button in the center of each white circle.

5 Working from the back of the wreath front, cut small slits through the blue felt behind each leaf shape, making sure you don't cut through the leaf itself.

6 Pin the 25-inch (63.5 cm) felt strip to the inside edge of the wreath front, leaving the raw edges exposed. Stitch the two together with blue thread, and follow these same steps to attach the strip to the wreath back. There will

be a small open flap where the strip overlaps its starting point. Hand-stitch this closed before moving onto the next step.

Tip: When you're pinning a straight shape to a curved shape, try turning the rim up as you pin the two together.

7 Pin and stitch the 50-inch (127 cm) strip to the outside edge of the wreath front.

8 Fill the leaves from behind with stuffing. Try using a chopstick or a knitting needle to push the stuffing into the slits you cut in step 5.

9 Pin the strip to the outside edge of the wreath back. Stitch the two pieces together, leaving a hole for stuffing. Hand-stitch the flap closed where the strip overlaps its starting point.

10 Stuff the wreath.

11 Cut a 1 x 6-inch (2.5 x 15.2 cm) strip from the dark green felt with shears. To strengthen the strip, add a couple of lines of blue stitching down the center of it. Pin the strip in place in the center of the hole you left for stuffing, between the strip and the wreath back and with the ends extending into the wreath. Pin and stitch the hole closed, catching the ends of the hanger in the seam. Add a few extra lines of stitching over the hanger ends to secure it.

Decorations •

These hand-Stitched Gift Tags, with backs you can write on, won't end up in the pile of gift-wrap on Christmas morning.

Stitched Gift Tags

DESIGNER: CATHY ZIEGELE

WHAT YOU NEED

(for the floral tag)

Basic sewing kit (page 9)

Templates (page 125)

Light green, light blue, light yellow, and blue-green felt

Light yellow, blue-green, dark yellow, and light green embroidery floss

Fabric pen

Laser-jet printed fabric labels

Hole punch

Yellow ribbon

WHAT YOU DO

1 Cut one floral tag template shape from light green felt and one from blue-green felt. Cut the border template shape from light blue felt and the flower template shapes from light yellow felt.

Tip: You may be able to create these shapes or similar ones with a die-cut system.

2 Cut two leaf shapes from the blue-green felt.

3 Baste the border onto the top edge of the tag front, lining up the straight edges and corners. Following the curve of the border, sew a single-threaded running stitch (page 11), using the blue-green floss for the running stitch and light green for the threaded part. Create light yellow French knots inside each curve.

4 Draw a small dot in the center of each flower with your fabric pen. Arrange your flowers on the tag front, making sure the leaf placement will not interfere with the stems and buds.

5 With light green floss, stitch a line from between the petals half way to the center dot to give more definition to each flower center. Stitch several blue-green French knots in the center of each flower. Sew a "V" in each petal with the dark yellow floss.

6 Cut tiny triangles out of the yellow felt. Cut a "V" into one end to create the bud. Using the photo as a reference, arrange the buds on the tag front and stitch around the lower half with light green floss, working your way down to the tip.

7 Create light green stems in backstitch from the buds to the flowers, making a small stem and French knot along the way. Stitch dark yellow stamens and light blue French knots from the center of each bud. Attach the leaves with light green floss.

8 Sew a printed fabric label to the tag back with French knots. With wrong sides together, baste the tag front and back together, and then use light green floss to blanket-stitch around the edges, making a detour for the hole you will punch for the hanging loop.

9 Punch a hole just in from the top edge of the tag, and feed the hanging loop through.

continued

These lovely keepsakes can be a gift tag one year and become the most beautiful ornament on the tree the next.

For the Diamond Tag:

1 Using the templates, cut the tag front and back from the light green and the blue-green felt.

2 Cut seven diamond shapes from the blue-green felt. Arrange and baste six in place on the tag front. Sew a running stitch in contrasting thread both inside and outside the diamonds. Create French knots at each point of the diamonds.

3 Cut a strip of light green felt a bit wider than the last diamond. Center the last diamond on the strip, and then baste this onto the tag back, leaving space for the hole you will punch. Sew a running stitch inside and outside the diamond using contrasting thread.

4 Attach a printed label using French knots. With the wrong sides together, baste the tag front and back together, and then blanket-stitch around the outside edge with light green floss.

5 Punch a hole, and feed the hanging loop through.

Little Birds Garland

DESIGNER: LISA JORDAN

The tiny flock in this
Little Birds Garland
will add charm to your
home year round.

Little Birds Garland

WHAT YOU NEED

Basic sewing kit (page 9)

Templates (page 117)

2 pieces of felt in cream and blue, each measuring 8 x 10 inches (20.3 x 25.4 cm)

Embroidery floss in coordinating and accent colors

12 buttons, preferably shank or 2-hole buttons measuring roughly ¼ inch (6 mm) or smaller

Stuffing (scrap wool, polyester stuffing, or other)

Jute, hemp twine, or narrow ribbon for the hanging loop, at least 20 inches (50.8 cm) long

Fabric glue (optional)

WHAT YOU DO

1 Copy and cut out the templates, and arrange them on the felt, making good use of space so you are able to cut all the pieces you need. You'll need two body shapes and two wing shapes for each bird on your garland. Cut three birds from cream and three birds from blue.

2 Organize your birds, putting two body pieces, two wings, and two buttons together into groups, alternating the color of the bird body and the wing color. You'll be decorating all of the pieces before you begin to assemble the garland.

3 Place a wing shape on a body shape. With three strands of embroidery floss, stitch the wing on using a whipstitch or running stitch. Using a contrasting color of embroidery floss, make a few decorative stitches to suggest feathers. Sew the small button eye onto the bird securely. Repeat the process for the other side of the bird, arranging the wing and eye so these features match up neatly when the two pieces are sewn together.

Tip: Tack the wing piece down with a dot of fabric glue to keep it from moving around while you sew.

4 Repeat this process for the remaining birds, creating six pairs of decorated bird pieces.

5 Sew one pair of matching bird pieces together with a length of three-strand embroidery floss that is roughly 30 inches (76.2 cm) long. Starting at the bottom center of the belly, use a blanket stitch to stitch around to the center top of the bird. Stop sewing when your bird hangs level when dangled from the remaining floss. Before going forward, stuff the tail of the bird while it's still accessible.

6 Tie a 3-inch-long (7.6 cm) loop at the top of your hemp, jute, or ribbon, and knot it securely. Tie a knot roughly ¾ inch (1.9 cm) down from the top knot. These knots will be secured inside the bird and will hold each bird in place on the garland.

7 Slide the half-sewn bird over the knot on the garland and sew over it, encasing it inside the stitching. Continue sewing around the bird until there is a ¾-inch (1.9 cm) opening left, and finish stuffing the bird.

Tip: If you're using narrow ribbon, be sure to make a large enough knot so it doesn't slip through the stitch.

8 Finish sewing the bird, concealing the bottom knot inside the stitching. Tie a knot in your embroidery floss and hide it to finish.

9 The remainder of the string, jute, or ribbon will be hanging down from the bottom of the bird. Tie two more knots below the first bird—one 1 inch (2.5 cm) down and one 1¾ inches (4.4 cm) down from the belly—and continue sewing birds to the garland. Repeat the process until all the birds are sewn to the string. When you reach the last bird, trim the bottom knot so that it doesn't protrude from the bird.

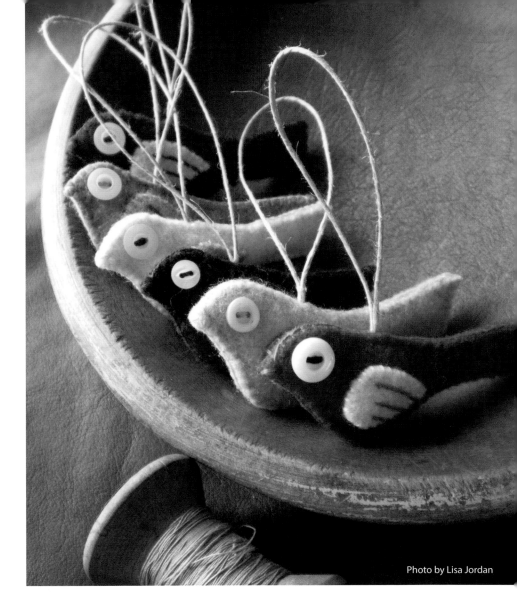

Photo by Lisa Jordan

Variation Idea:

These little birdies also make darling ornaments if you'd rather not string them all in a row. Simply add a hanging loop at the top of each bird.

String together simple felt spirals and beads to create this cheerful and sweet Christmas Candy Garland.

Christmas Candy Garland

DESIGNER: ESTHER COAR

WHAT YOU DO

1 Cut several 1/2 x 9-inch (1.3 x 22.9 cm) strips of red and white felt. You'll need two red strips and one white strip for each candy.

2 Stack the strips together with the white strip on top, carefully lining up the long edges.

3 Roll the strips, keeping the red strips on the outside.

Tip: To create a solid center, begin rolling with one color felt and then add in the second color.

4 Use two straight pins to hold the candy together by pinning through the center.

5 Stitch the end of the strips together to keep them from unrolling. In a pinch, you can skip this step: when the candies are strung on the garland, pressure from the beads will keep them rolled.

6 Using the heavy-duty needle, thread the candies onto the waxed thread and alternate with beads, making sure the needle goes through the stitched end of felt and the candy center. Since your needle will have to travel through many layers of felt, use your pliers to pull the needle through, or try pushing the needle against a solid object to get it through the candy.

7 Tie hanging loops at each end of the garland.

WHAT YOU NEED

Basic sewing kit (page 9)

Red and white felt

Matching thread

Long heavy-duty needle

Waxed thread, 2 feet (.6 m) longer than your desired garland length

An assortment of beads

Pliers

Decorations •

Start saving all your odds and ends for this easy, no-sew felt Scrap Wreath.

Scrap Wreath

DESIGNER: KATHY SHELDON

WHAT YOU NEED

Wire coat hanger

Metal cutters

Scraps of felt in various colors (amount will depend on size of wreath)

Felted sweater material (see page 8 for instructions)

Duct tape

Ribbon, twine, or felt

WHAT YOU DO

1 Bend the wire coat hanger into a circle. Cut the circle open about 3 inches (7.6 cm) down one side from the hanger's hook.

2 Cut the purchased felt and felted sweater material into rough 4-inch (10.2 cm) squares.

Tip: This wreath will look best if your squares aren't exact and you vary their sizes a bit.

3 Sort your felt squares by color into piles to make it easier to distribute colors evenly around the wreath.

4 Fold one square from the first pile in half to form a triangle. Use the cut end of the long section of the hanger to poke a hole through the center of the triangle from the first pile, and slide the fabric up snug against the hook at the top of the hanger.

5 Continue adding squares of felt and felted material to the wreath in this manner, following any combination of colors you find pleasing. Don't align the corners of the triangles perfectly; instead vary their arrangement to achieve a nice full effect.

6 When you reach the cut end of the hanger, begin adding triangles to the short end of the wire, pushing them up against the hook. Once the hanger is completely full of felt, tape the cut ends of the hanger together securely, and then redistribute the felted pieces to hide the taped section.

7 If your wreath has become a bit bent out of shape, gently bend it back into a nice round circle. Cover the exposed part of the hanger with ribbon, twine, or felt.

This garland of felt and fabric *Fa La La La Leaves* will
add a sparkle of festivity wherever you place it!

Fa La La La Leaves

DESIGNER: CONSTANÇA CABRAL

WHAT YOU NEED

Basic sewing kit (page 9)

Template (page 117)

Assorted scraps of felt in white, red, turquoise, and teal

Assorted scraps of printed cotton fabric in white, red, and turquoise

Photos by Constança Cabral

WHAT YOU DO

1 Using the template, cut leaves from the felt and fabric. When you cut the leaves out of the printed fabric, fold the fabric over before you cut to create pairs.

2 After cutting your fabric leaves, align them wrong sides together, and press each pair using a hot iron. This will make the leaves stick to each other, making the sewing step much easier.

3 Stitching through the middle of each leaf, feed the leaves through the sewing machine one after another without breaking the threads after stitching each leaf (this process is also called chaining). These threads will connect the leaves into a garland. Work in a random fashion, alternating colors and also alternating between felt and fabric.

4 Tie a knot at each end of the garland, and cut off the thread.

These no-sew **Snowflake Coasters**,
created with thick industrial wool felt,
are fun to make and surprisingly mod.

Snowflake Coasters

DESIGNER: ELLEN LUCKETT BAKER

WHAT YOU NEED

Template (page 123)

Cardboard or plastic pattern sheet

Craft knife with sharp blade

Rotary cutter

3mm blue wool felt, 8 x 8 inches (20.3 x 20.3 cm)

White wool felt in any thickness, 8 x 8 inches (20.3 x 20.3 cm)

Masking tape

Craft glue and paintbrush

WHAT YOU DO

1 Using the template, cut out a cardboard or plastic pattern piece. Use the craft knife to cut out the snowflake design on your pattern piece.

2 Using a rotary cutter, cut the blue and white felt pieces into four 4 x 4-inch (10.2 x 10.2 cm) squares for a total of eight felt squares.

3 Line up your template over a blue felt square, and secure it in place with masking tape. Carefully cut out the snowflake design with your craft knife, being sure to leave clean edges. Repeat with the remaining blue felt squares.

4 Brush glue onto the back of a blue felt square, and glue it on top of one of the white squares. Repeat this process for all four coasters.

5 Use scissors to round the corners of your squares, using the project photo or the template as a guide.

Make a shining statement: trim your tree with a simple *String of Stars*.

String of Stars

DESIGNER: CATARINA FILIPE

WHAT YOU NEED

Basic sewing kit (page 9)

Template (page 125)

Fabric pen

White felt, ½ yard (.5 m)

Red cotton cord, 70 inches (177.8 cm)

Red embroidery floss

WHAT YOU DO

1 Using the template and a fabric pen, trace and cut 20 stars, or enough for 10 pairs.

2 Make a loop and tie a knot at one end of the cord.

3 Measure 4 inches (10.2 cm) from the loop and tie a knot. Pin one pair of star shapes in place on the cord with wrong sides together, sandwiching the cord in between and positioning the widest point of the star so it touches the knot.

4 Using the red floss, blanket-stitch around the outside edge of the star. Tie a knot at the other end of the star, where the cord extends from between the star layers. Measure 4 inches (10.2 cm) from this knot and tie another one. Repeat this process until you've added all 10 stars to the cord.

5 To end the garland, hide a final, bigger knot in the last star or create another tied hanging loop.

Upcycle! Turn old sweaters into holiday decorations with fast, no-sew *Thrifted Holiday Trees*.

Thrifted Holiday Trees

DESIGNER: ELLEN LUCKETT BAKER

WHAT YOU NEED

Templates (page 125)

Felted wool sweaters (see page 8 for felting instructions)

Thin wire, approximately 10 inches (25.4 cm)

Bead or wood star for the tree top

Wire cutters or heavy-duty scissors

Glue (optional)

WHAT YOU DO

1 Using the template provided, cut the felted sweaters into circles. Cut two sweater circles of each size.

2 Bend your wire at one end, and slip the sweater circles onto the wire by poking a hole through the center. Begin with the largest circles first, and work your way up to the top, using smaller circles as you go.

3 Wrap a bead or star at the top, and bend the wire around. Snip the excess wire.

4 If you'd like, add some glue between the layers for added stability.

Fa la la la stockings

Here, the  traditional holiday stocking gets a modern update. These simple creations—even when empty—are full of holiday cheer. Made of brightly colored felt  and a couple of stray scraps, they can herald the season more happily and completely than any tree or snowflake or fruitcake.

Reverse appliqué is the sweet
secret behind this
Oopsy Daisies stocking.

Oopsy Daisies

DESIGNER: AMANDA CARESTIO

WHAT YOU NEED

Basic sewing kit (page 9)

Templates (page 120)

Blue felt, 1/2 yard (.5 m)

Fat quarter of cotton fabric

Fabric pen

Light green thread

Light green embroidery floss

WHAT YOU DO

1 Enlarge and cut out the stocking template. Cut the petal shapes out of the paper template.

2 Use the stocking template to cut out two stocking shapes. Flip the stocking front over, turn the cut-out template over, and trace the flower shapes onto the back of the stocking front with the fabric marker. Cut out the flower petals.

3 Cut three 4-inch (10.2 cm) squares from the fat quarter. Pin the squares to the back of the stocking front behind each flower shape.

Tip: If you're using a fabric that has stripes or any type of linear pattern, make sure the pattern runs in the same direction behind each flower.

4 Top stitch around the petals with light green thread, and trim off the excess fabric.

5 With the light green embroidery floss, create several French knots in each flower center. Use running stitches to create tendrils extending out from the center of each flower.

6 Create the hanging loop by cutting a 1/2 x 8-inch (1.3 x 20.3 cm) strip from the fat quarter and a 3/4 x 8-inch (1.9 x 20.3 cm) strip of blue felt. Sew the fabric strip onto the center of the felt strip.

7 Pin the stocking front to the stocking back with right sides facing, sandwiching the hanging loop at the top right about 3/4 inch (1.9 cm) down from the top stocking edge, with the loop to the inside and the raw edges sticking out. Stitch around the outside edge of the stocking, leaving the top edge open.

8 Create the cuff by cutting two 3 1/2 x 7-inch (8.9 x 17.8 cm) strips from the fat quarter. Fold under the bottom long edge of each strip twice and stitch along the edge.

9 With the right sides facing, stitch the front short edge of the cuff together. Stitch the back short edge of the cuff together, stopping halfway. Fold in the remaining raw edges and stitch down each side; this will create a split seam in the back of the cuff where the hanging loop will fit.

10 With both the cuff and the stocking inside out, pin the cuff around the top edge of the stocking, making sure the split seam is lined up over the hanging loop. Stitch around the top edge.

11 Turn the stocking right side out and fold the cuff over.

Stockings

Add a touch of whimsy to your holiday décor with the bright polka dots and curled toe of this Elfin stocking.

Elfin

DESIGNER: REBEKAH J. THOMPSON

WHAT YOU NEED

Basic sewing kit (page 9)

Templates (page 119)

Light pink felt, 1/2 yard (.5 m)

Scraps of green, light green, and yellow felt

Light pink and dark pink thread

WHAT YOU DO

1 Using the templates, cut two light pink stocking shapes, two green cuff shapes, and two 3/4 x 6-inch (1.9 x 15.2 cm) strips, one in light green and one in light pink.

2 Cut four 3-inch-diameter (7.6 cm) circles from light green felt and six 1-inch-diameter (2.5 cm) circles from yellow.

3 Lay out your stocking pieces, deciding which way you'd like it to hang—either with the toe to the left or right. Start arranging the dots and circles on the stocking front in a staggered fashion. Place two large circles overhanging the edge of the body. Pin each circle down, and trim off the part of the circles that extend past the edge by following the shape of the stocking.

4 With contrasting thread, straight stitch an "X" into the middle of each small circle, being sure to backstitch. Slowly zigzag-stitch around the edge of each large circle, beginning and ending with a couple of backstitches.

5 Pin the two loop pieces together, and zigzag-stitch them together into one double layer strip.

6 Pin your stocking front and back together with right sides facing. Change your thread to match the body, and sew around the edges, leaving the top open.

7 Pin the two cuff pieces together with right sides facing. Sew down the front edge. Leaving the right sides together, insert the folded loop between the two cuff pieces at the back of the cuff, placing the loops about 3/8 inch (9.5 mm) down from the top edge and with the ends sticking out. Sew down the back edge of the cuff, catching the loop ends in the seam.

8 With your stocking and cuff inside out, place the cuff around the top of the stocking, matching the seams and top edges. Make sure the loop seam is on the heel seam. Pin the cuff in place, and sew them together around the top edge starting at one seam. Turn your stocking right side out, and fold down the cuff.

Layer on the details and put some *Paisley Power* to work this holiday.

Paisley Power

DESIGNER: CATHY ZIEGELE

WHAT YOU NEED

Basic sewing kit (page 9)

Templates (page 120)

Light green and blue felt, 12 x 18-inch (30.5 x 45.7 cm) sheet each

Purple, light blue, red, green, and chartreuse felt scraps, at least 4 x 5 inches (10.2 x 12.7 cm)

Fusible bond iron-on fabric

Embroidery floss in various colors

Thread to match stocking and paisleys

Beads or sequins (optional)

Pink ribbon, ³/₄ inch (1.9 cm) wide

WHAT YOU DO

1 Using the templates, cut one stocking back piece from the blue felt, one stocking front piece from light green, and one toe and heel piece from chartreuse.

2 After you've decided on your layout and colors, cut the paisley shapes out following the templates, and baste them to the stocking front. Stack the paisley pieces, using the photo as a guide.

3 Attach the pieces with a variety of embroidery stitches: blanket stitch, blanket stitch with French knots in between or on top, single-threaded running stitch (page 11) with French knots in alternating colors, double-threaded running stitch (page 10), lazy daisy stitch, and a zigzag stitch with French knots in alternating colors. Intersperse beads or sequins for added sparkle.

4 After you've embellished the front, iron on a stabilizing fabric to cover the threads and strengthen the area where you'll cut the hole for the ribbon hanger.

5 Baste the stocking front to the back to prevent shifting. For added strength, machine stitch the pieces together before moving to the next step. Sew the pieces together with a running stitch.

6 Sew a ring of stitching around the place where you'd like to place the hole for the ribbon hanger, stitching through both the stocking front and back. Cut the hole carefully and insert the ribbon.

Gold beads, red diamonds,
and a super curly toe give
this **Jester** just the right mix
of luster and fun.

Jester

DESIGNER: CATHY ZIEGELE

WHAT YOU NEED

Basic sewing kit (page 9)

Templates (page 119)

Light green felt, two 12 x 18-inch (30.5 x 45.7 cm) sheets

Dark red felt, 9 x 12-inch (22.9 x 30.5 cm)

Fabric pen

Metallic gold and light green embroidery floss

6/0 gold glass beads

Fusible bond fabric (optional)

Hole punch

Light green ribbon

WHAT YOU DO

1 Using the template, cut two stocking bodies from the light green felt.

2 Cut 12 diamonds from the dark red felt, and arrange them on the front of the stocking body. Carefully baste them down using regular sewing thread.

3 Mark lines down the center of each row of diamonds with your fabric pen and a ruler. Sew a backstitch with the gold floss along these lines, one row at a time. Then work your way across the diamonds until you've created a cross in each one.

4 Using the light green floss, place a bead at the points of all the diamonds—except the outer edges—and randomly down the boot of the stocking all the way to the toe. Tie off each bead with a secure knot and trim the thread.

5 To strengthen the hole for the hanging ribbon, cut the fusible bonding fabric just big enough to cover the inside threads and the area where you're planning to cut the hole. Iron the fabric to the felt.

Tip: Use a dry iron for this step and work over a thick towel. It might be a good idea to experiment first with scraps.

6 With wrong sides together, baste the stocking front to the back using sewing thread. Blanket-stitch around the outside edge with light green floss, stringing on a gold bead before you make each stitch.

7 At the outside of the tip of the curly toe, place a few beads to make it look as if the toe is separate. In the center of the toe loop, place a bead in every other stitch to prevent crowding.

8 Sew beads across the top front using beads and the blanket stitch.

9 At the top right corner of the stocking and working through both stocking layers, sew a circle that's larger than your hole punch to strengthen the hole you will make for the ribbon hanger. Punch the hole, and thread in some ribbon for the hanger.

Tired of red and green?
Trade in poinsettias
for a Perky Pansy
this year.

Perky Pansy

DESIGNER: REBEKAH J. THOMPSON

WHAT YOU DO

1 Using the templates, cut two stocking pieces from white felt, two cuff pieces from light blue, and two 3/4 x 6-inch (1.9 x 15.2 cm) strips of felt in different colors for the loop. Also, cut out the leaves and the three different flower shapes you'll need to create the pansy.

2 Lay the stocking front in the direction you want the finished stocking to hang. Place the leaves in the middle of the stocking slightly offset to one side, pin them in place, and sew up each leaf to create a vein. Stack the three flowers on top of the leaves, and, starting in the middle of the smallest flower, sew up each of the four petals, stitching through all three flower shapes at once.

3 Place the stocking back on top of the front, with right sides together and matching the edges, and pin them in place. If any of the petals are close to the edge of the stocking, fold them back and pin them so that they don't get sewn into the seam allowance. Sew around the edge of the body, leaving the top open.

4 Stack the two loop strips, and sew down the middle with a zigzag stitch. Place the two cuff pieces together with right sides facing, and sew down one side edge. Leaving the cuff pieces inside out, fold the loop strip in half, and insert it into the opposite side of the cuff so that the loop is 3/8 inch (9.5 mm) down from the top edge and the ends are sticking out. Sew down this edge, catching the loop ends in the seam.

5 With both pieces inside out, place the cuff piece over and around the top opening of the stocking—matching the seams and top edges and lining up the loop seam with the heel seam—and pin them together. Sew around the top edge, without sewing the loop into the seam.

6 Turn the stocking right side out, and fold down the cuff.

WHAT YOU NEED

Basic sewing kit (page 9)

Templates (page 120)

White felt, 1/2 yard (.5 m)

Three shades of blue and green felt sheets, each 9 x 12 inches (22.9 x 30.5 cm)

Little scraps of cotton peek through felt windows to create dimension on this *Leaf & Vine* stocking.

Leaf & Vine

DESIGNER: AMANDA CARESTIO

WHAT YOU NEED

Basic sewing kit (page 9)

Templates (page 119)

Dark purple felt, 1/3 yard (.3 m)

Gray felt, two 9 x 12-inch (22.9 x 30.5 cm) sheets

Scraps of gray print cotton fabric

Purple and white sewing thread

WHAT YOU DO

1 Using the template, cut out two dark purple stocking shapes.

2 Trace the vine shape from the template onto the gray felt. Cut out a 1/4-inch (6 mm) strip along the line, piecing strips together if needed to create the total length of the vine. You can hide the strip seams later by placing leaves on top of them.

3 Pin the strip (or strips) in place on the stocking front. Stitch through the center of the strip with purple thread.

4 Cut five leaf shapes from gray felt using the leaf template. Fold each leaf in half and cut out the middle, leaving at least a 1/4-inch (6 mm) border at each edge.

5 Lay out your second piece of felt with the cotton fabric on top, right side up. Place the felt leaf cutouts from the previous step on top of the cotton fabric and pin them in place.

6 With purple thread, stitch around the outside of each felt leaf, stitching through the top layer of felt, the cotton fabric, and the bottom layer of felt. Stitch through the center of each leaf. Cut out the leaves, using the top felt leaf shape as a guide.

7 Pin the leaves to the stocking front, placing them along the vine. Stitch the leaves in place following the stitch lines from the previous step. You can sew all around the shapes or leave parts free for more dimension. When you're attaching the leaves that extend past the stocking shape, do not stitch all the way to the edge of the stocking.

8 Starting at the top right and working your way around to the top left, stitch around the leaves and vine, first in purple thread (about 1/4 inch [6 mm] from the shapes) and then in white thread (about 1/2 inch [1.3 cm] from the shapes).

9 Pin the stocking front to the stocking back with wrong sides together. Fold over the leaves that extend past the stocking and pin them to themselves. Stitch around the outside edge of the stocking, using a 1/4-inch (6 mm) seam allowance and white thread. Next, stitch around the top edge of the stocking with white thread.

10 From the gray felt, cut two 1/2 x 8-inch (1.3 x 20.3 cm) strips. Stitch a single line down the center of each strip with purple thread. Sandwich the strips between the stocking front and back, and stitch in place several times to secure them. Tie the strips in a knot.

Just Let It Snow. This cute critter—created with a mixture of felt and felted sweater—is ready for a snowball fight.

Let It Snow

DESIGNER: CATHY GAUBERT

WHAT YOU NEED

Basic sewing kit (page 9)

Templates (page 118)

Gray felted sweater wool, two 10 x 16-inch (25.4 x 40.6 cm) pieces

White wool felt, one 6 x 6-inch (15.2 x 15.2 cm) piece and one 2 x 8-inch (5 x 20.3 cm) piece (for the cuff)

Green wool felt, 2 x 2 inches (5 x 5 cm)

Gray wool felt, 2 x 3 inches (5 x 7.6 cm)

Red wool felt, one 3 x 6-inch (7.6 x 15.2 cm) piece and one 1 x 8-inch (2.5 x 20.3 cm) piece (for the hanger)

Red, white, gray, and green thread

White and black embroidery floss

WHAT YOU DO

1 Using the template, cut two stocking shapes from the gray felted sweater wool. If possible, cut the pieces so the ribbing at the bottom of the sweater is the top of the stocking.

2 Use the other templates to cut the pom-pom, head, hand, and snowflake shapes from white felt, a hat shape from green, a scarf shape from gray, and one coat and arm shape from red.

3 Using the photo as a guide, begin building the bear's image on the front of the stocking. Set aside the back of the stocking for now.

4 Stitch right inside the edge of the coat shape to attach it to the stocking. Position the sleeve, and stitch right inside the left edge, stopping about 1/2 inch (1.3 cm) from the cuff. Slide the paw under the edge of the sleeve and continue stitching to catch the paw under the sleeve's end; the paw itself will stay loose.

5 Stack the snowballs onto the paw. Starting at the top of the smallest snowball, stitch through the middle of all three.

6 Position the scarf on top of the neck of the coat and stitch it in place, leaving 1/2 inch (1.3 cm) of the end of the scarf unstitched. Snip slits in the end of the scarf to create fringe.

7 Position and then stitch the head and hat shapes in place above the scarf.

8 Fold the pom-pom shape in half twice to make a pie shape. Stitch back and forth through the center to secure, and then cut little snips into the loose edges. Hand-stitch the pom-pom to the top of the hat.

9 Using two strands of black embroidery floss, make a French knot for each eye and then satin stitch the nose. With three strands of white floss, make stitches of varying lengths to add dimension to the face and paw.

10 Randomly attach the snowballs to the front of the stocking with little floss knots.

11 Using a rotary cutter or scissors, scallop the bottom edge of the white cuff piece. Place it on top of the stocking, and then trim the sides to fit. Pin it in place and stitch across the top and the bottom.

12 Scallop both long edges of the red hanging strip. Fold the strip in half to form a loop. Pin it in place so the edge of the loop will be caught in the seam of the stocking.

13 Pin the front and back of the stocking together, with right sides facing out. Starting on the top side near the loop, stitch slightly inside the edge of the stocking all the way around until you reach the other side.

Stockings

This stocking's bold design makes your holidays Cheery & Bright and is a great way to use up felt scraps.

Cheery & Bright

DESIGNER: LAURA HOWARD

WHAT YOU DO

1 Cut out two identical stocking shapes from the turquoise felt using the template.

2 Create the first bauble starting with the smallest circle first. Using the template, cut a small felt circle from your scraps. Using this shape as a guide, cut out a slightly larger circle from a contrasting shade of felt, leaving a narrow border around the first circle as you cut.

3 Repeat this process until you've cut five circles in different sizes and colors. Use these circles as templates to cut two more sets of baubles. You should end up with three circles of each size in an assortment of bright, contrasting colors.

4 Layer the felt discs to make three piles of circles. Position them in a line down the right-hand side of the stocking front, about 3/4 inch (1.9 cm) in from the right edge.

5 Stitch each pile in place using two small stitches, sewing through the center of all five circles to form a small cross.

6 Place one button on each pile of circles, and sew it in place securely with a double thickness of thread.

7 Cut a 6-inch (15.2 cm) length of ribbon. Cut a small square of turquoise felt just wider than the ribbon.

8 Fold the ribbon in half, and position it at the top right-hand edge of the stocking back. Place the felt square over the ribbon ends so they are completely hidden.

9 Stitch around the edge of the square and from corner to corner to form an "X," sewing through the felt square, the stocking back, and the ribbon sandwiched between them.

10 Pin the stocking front and back together with wrong sides facing. Begin stitching about 1 inch (2.5 cm) from the top, and sew up to the top edge and then back down and around the whole stocking edge. Finish by sewing back down another inch (2.5 cm). This will help keep your knots and finishing hidden inside the stocking and strengthen the stocking opening.

11 With the pink embroidery thread, blanket-stitch around the outside edge of the stocking.

WHAT YOU NEED

Basic sewing kit (page 9)

Templates (page 119)

Turquoise felt, two 9 x 12-inch (22.9 x 30.5 cm) sheets

Scraps of felt in assorted bright colors

Turquoise thread

Three buttons

Turquoise ribbon, 3/4 inch (1.9 cm) wide

Pink embroidery floss

Create the perfect treat-catching
Pet Stocking for your favorite
furry, feathered, or fishy friend.

Pet Stockings

DESIGNER: REBEKAH J. THOMPSON

WHAT YOU NEED

Basic sewing kit (page 9)

Templates (page 118)

Assorted felt, two to three 9 x 12-inch (22.9 x 30.5 cm) sheets

Thread to match stocking and elements

WHAT YOU DO

1 Using the templates, cut the following: the design elements, two stocking shapes, two cuff pieces, and two $3/4$ x 5-inch (1.9 x 12.7 cm) strips of felt for the hanging loop. Also, cut out your pet's initial, making sure that it's no more than $1^1/_2$ inches (3.8 cm) tall and that it fits on the larger design element.

2 With the stocking front laid out in the direction you want the toe to point, begin laying out the design elements, adjusting as needed so the cuff can fold down without blocking your design. Pin all the elements in place (except for the initial), and then stitch around the outside edge of each shape.

3 When the stocking front is complete, place the stocking back on top of the front, with right sides facing and matching all edges. Pin your two layers together, and sew around the perimeter of the stocking, leaving the top open.

4 Sandwich the two loop pieces together, and sew down the middle to make one loop strip.

5 Stack the two cuff pieces together—one on top of the other with right sides facing—and sew one side edge. Fold the loop in half, and insert it in the opposite, open edge of the cuff about $3/8$ inch (9.5 mm) down from the top of the cuff and with both loop ends sticking out the side. Sew this edge of the cuff, catching the loop ends in the seam.

6 Place the cuff over and around the top of the stocking—both should be inside out—matching the seams and making sure the loop seam of the cuff matches the heel seam of the stocking. Pin the two together, and sew around the top edge.

7 Turn your stocking right side out, and fold down the cuff. With felt glue, attach the initial onto the main design, and let the stocking dry following the manufacturer's directions.

These *Simple Stripes* have attitude. Imagine a whole row in bright, contrasting colors.

Simple Stripes

DESIGNER: REBEKAH J. THOMPSON

WHAT YOU NEED

Basic sewing kit (page 9)

Templates (page 120)

Orange felt, 1/2 yard (.5 m)

Pink felt, 9 x 12-inch (22.9 x 30.5 cm)

Light pink and orange thread

WHAT YOU DO

1 Using the templates, cut two orange stocking pieces, two pink cuff pieces, and one pink heel shape. For the stripes, cut seven pink $1^1/_2$ x 6-inch (3.8 x 15.2 cm) strips, and two $^3/_4$ x 6-inch (1.9 x 15.2 cm) strips—one pink and one orange—for the hanging loop.

2 Lay the stocking front down—with the toe pointing in whichever direction you'd like—and begin placing the stripes on top. Space the stripes as evenly as possible. The stripe across the heel may not reach the whole way, but the heel piece will cover it up. When you're happy with the placement, pin all the stripes to the stocking front.

3 Using the light pink thread and either a straight or decorative stitch, sew along the edge of each stripe. Stitch the heel piece in place overlapping the heel stripe.

4 Place the stocking back on top of the front, with right sides facing and matching the edges. Pin the pieces together, and sew around the edges of the stocking, catching the edges of the stripes and the heel piece in the seams and leaving the top open.

5 Stack the cuff pieces together, and stitch down the front edge. Open the cuff, and sew a decorative stitch following the curved edge from end to end. Stack the two loop pieces, and use the same decorative stitch to sew them together down the middle.

6 Fold the cuff back so that right sides are facing in. Fold the loop in half, and insert it in the opposite, open edge of the cuff about $^3/_8$ inch (9.5 mm) down from the top of the cuff and with both loop ends sticking out the side. Sew this edge of the cuff, catching the loop ends in the seam.

7 Place the cuff over and around the top of the stocking—both should be inside out—matching the seams and making sure the loop seam of the cuff matches the heel seam of the stocking. Pin the two together, and sew around the top edge.

8 Turn your stocking right side out, and fold down the cuff.

Pretend these stockings are
Sorta Swedish heirlooms
your Aunt Anneke passed
down to you.

Sorta Swedish

DESIGNER: CINDY GREY

WHAT YOU NEED

Basic sewing kit (page 9)

Templates (page 118)

Red felt, two 9 x 12-inch (22.9 x 30.5 cm) sheets

White felt, two 9 x 12-inch (22.9 x 30.5 cm) sheets

White baby rickrack

Medium red rickrack

White and red embroidery floss

WHAT YOU DO

1 Starting with the red stocking first, use the template to cut out the stocking front from the red felt.

2 Pin the white rickrack around the edge of the stocking front, extending both ends 1 inch (2.5 cm) past the top edge of the stocking. Turn the extended piece of rickrack to the back, and sew the rickrack down using hand or machine stitches.

3 Using the templates, cut out each snowflake shape from white felt. Using one strand of white embroidery floss, attach the felt snowflakes to the stocking front.

4 With two strands of white embroidery floss, randomly add embroidered snowflakes to the stocking front.

5 To make the stocking hanger, cut a 1/2 x 5-inch (1.3 x 12.7 cm) strip of red felt and 5-inch (12.7 cm) length of white rickrack. Sew the rickrack to the center of the felt strip.

6 Pin the stocking front onto a piece of white felt. Do not cut the stocking back yet. Pin the stocking hanger on the right-hand side, between the red and white layers.

7 Sew through both layers with a row of white French knots between the stocking edge and the rickrack.

8 Following the shape of the stocking front, use pinking shears to cut the white felt, creating the stocking back.

9 To create the white stocking, follow steps 1 and 2, using white felt for the stocking front, red felt for the heart shapes, and red rickrack for the accents.

10 Using two strands of red floss, embroider snowflakes between the points of the rickrack.

11 With three strands of white floss, embroider small snowflakes on both hearts. Attach the hearts to the stocking front using three strands of red floss and the blanket stitch.

12 Finish the white stocking using the same steps you used to complete the red one.

USING *the* TEMPLATES

Here are all the templates necessary to make the projects in the book. To use them, just follow these guidelines:

For medium- to large-sized pattern pieces, enlarge the template to the appropriate percentage, and cut it out. Then pin the template onto the felt, and cut out the shape. For especially small or intricate shapes, cut out the paper template, pin it to the felt, and then use a water-soluble fabric marker to trace around it, directly onto the felt. Use the traced line for a cutting guide.

For patterns with embroidery designs, enlarge the embroidery design to the appropriate percentage and then transfer the design to your felt. If you're using a light felt color, you may be able to place the felt on top of the pattern and trace the stitch lines with a water-soluble marker. If your felt is too dark for the above method, enlarge the design, place it on top of the felt, and use a pin to poke small holes in the paper about $1/8$ inch (3 mm) apart along the design lines. Use a water-soluble marking pen to mark the fabric at each of the pinpricks. If the design is difficult to make out, remove the paper and use the same pen to connect the dots.

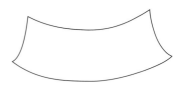

SILVER BELLS
Page 50 — copy at 200%

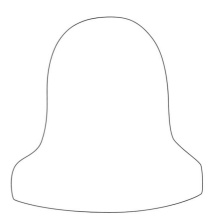

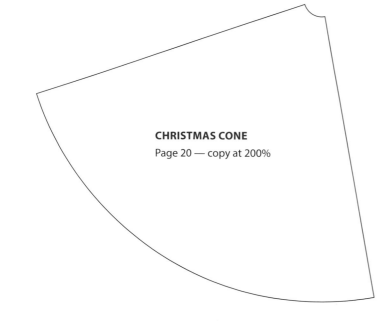

CHRISTMAS CONE
Page 20 — copy at 200%

PERCHING DOVE
Page 24 — copy at 200%

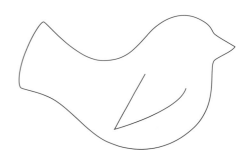

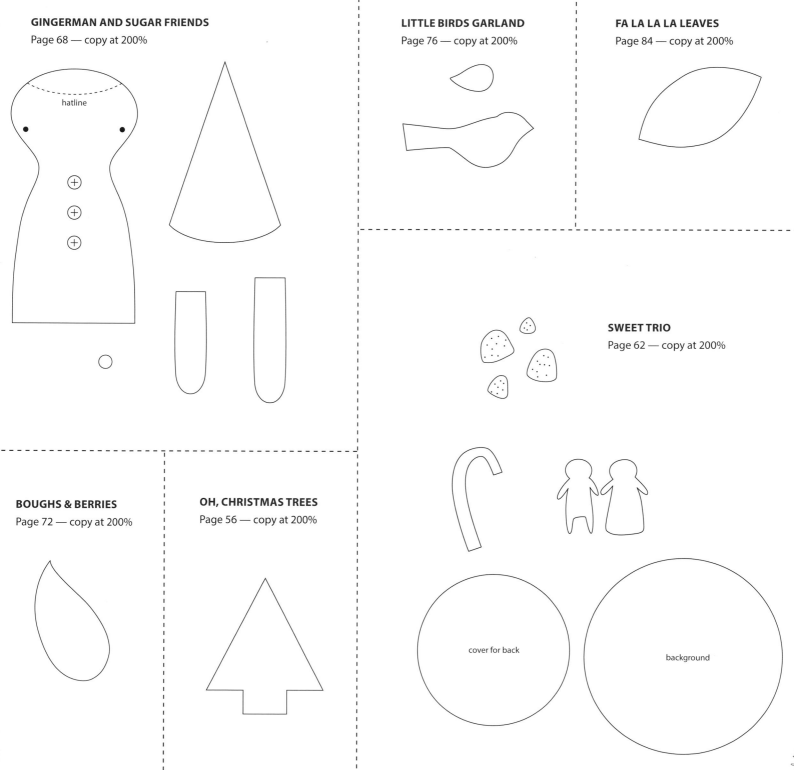

GINGERMAN AND SUGAR FRIENDS
Page 68 — copy at 200%

hatline

LITTLE BIRDS GARLAND
Page 76 — copy at 200%

FA LA LA LA LEAVES
Page 84 — copy at 200%

SWEET TRIO
Page 62 — copy at 200%

cover for back

background

BOUGHS & BERRIES
Page 72 — copy at 200%

OH, CHRISTMAS TREES
Page 56 — copy at 200%

Templates

LET IT SNOW

Page 106 — copy stocking at 400%, copy critter pieces at 200%

SORTA SWEDISH

Page 114 — copy at 300%

PET STOCKINGS

Page 110 — copy at 300%

cuff

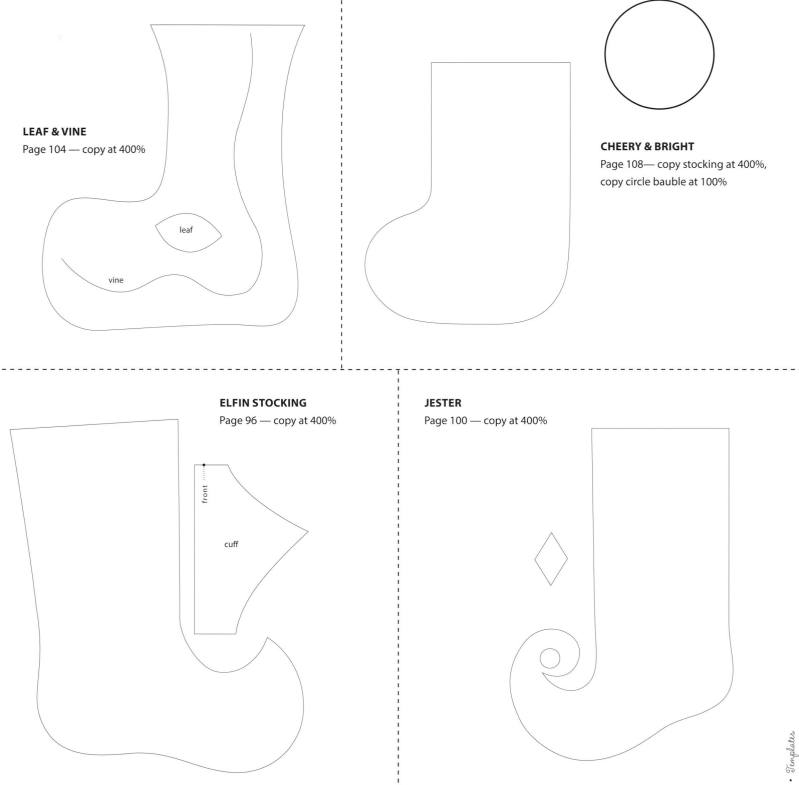

LEAF & VINE
Page 104 — copy at 400%

leaf

vine

CHEERY & BRIGHT
Page 108— copy stocking at 400%,
copy circle bauble at 100%

ELFIN STOCKING
Page 96 — copy at 400%

front

cuff

JESTER
Page 100 — copy at 400%

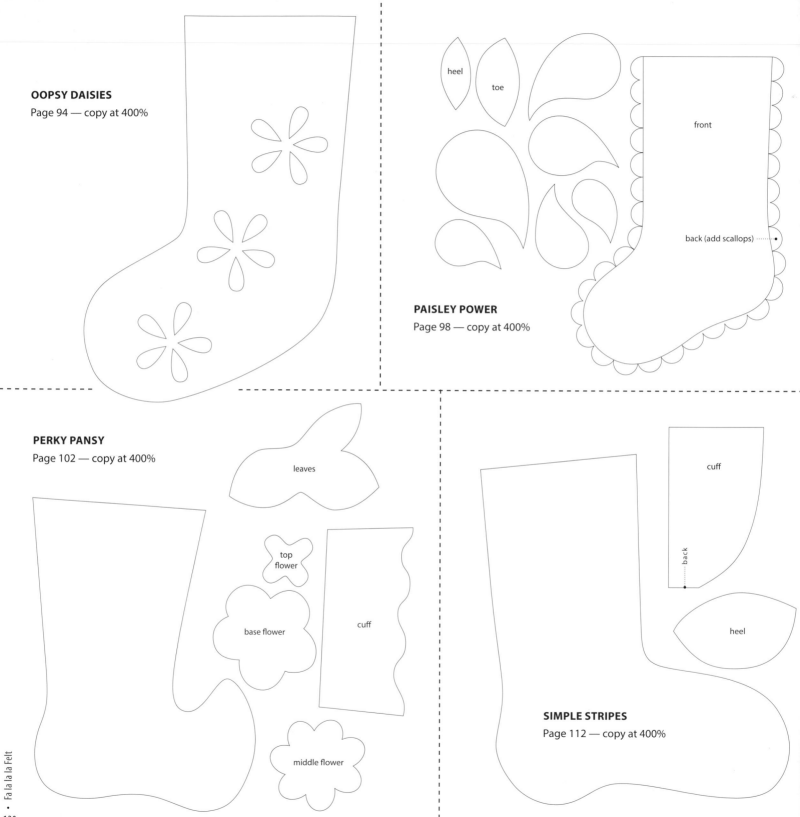

OOPSY DAISIES

Page 94 — copy at 400%

PAISLEY POWER

Page 98 — copy at 400%

heel

toe

front

back (add scallops)

PERKY PANSY

Page 102 — copy at 400%

leaves

top flower

base flower

cuff

middle flower

SIMPLE STRIPES

Page 112 — copy at 400%

cuff

back

heel

APPLE & PEAR ORNAMENTS
Page 32 — copy at 200%

WINTER CRITTER PORTRAITS
Page 16 — copy at 200%

frame

portrait

HOLIDAY HEARTS
Page 46 — copy at 200%

GINGERBREAD HOUSE
Page 26 — copy at 200%

Templates

LAYER PLAY
Page 52 — copy at 100%

FELT FLORA
Page 22 — copy at 200%

MERRY LITTLE ORNAMENT
Page 42 — copy at 200%

topper
(for variations)

HOLIDAY TOADSTOOLS
Page 28 — copy at 200%

STAR BRIGHT
Page 60 — copy at 200%

HOLIDAY HOOT
Page 48 — copy at 200%

BEADED TASSEL DROPS
Page 39— copy at 200%

body

center

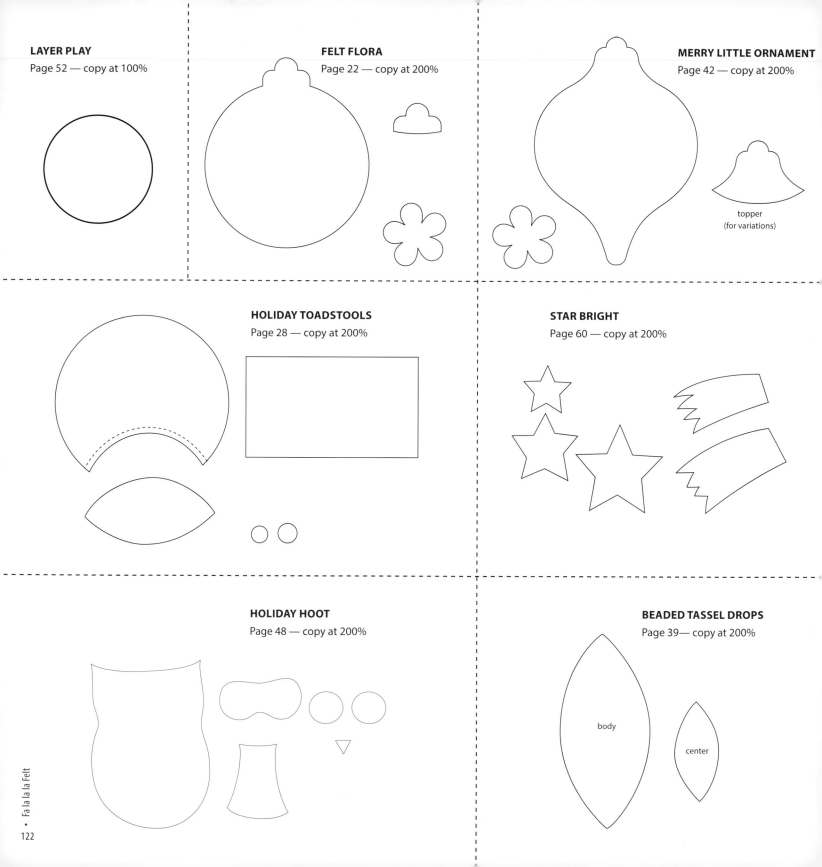

SNOWFLAKE BAUBLES
Page 14 — copy at 200%

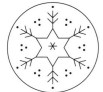

SNOWFLAKE COASTERS
Page 86 — copy at 200%

MINI STOCKINGS
Page 54 — copy at 200%

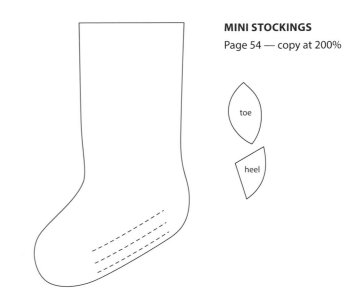

MINI STOCKING VARIATION — copy at 200%

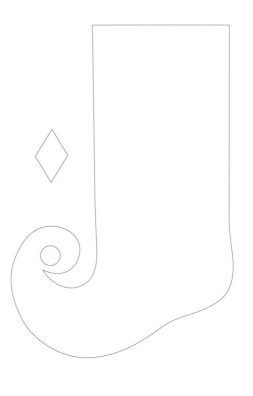

GOLDEN PARTRIDGES

Page 44 — copy at 200%

MATRYOSHKA DOLLS

Page 18 — copy at 200%

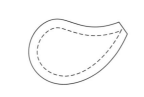

THREE WISE FISH

Page 34 — copy at 200%

SEW MERRY

Page 36 — copy at 200%

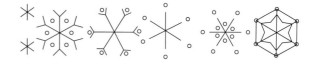

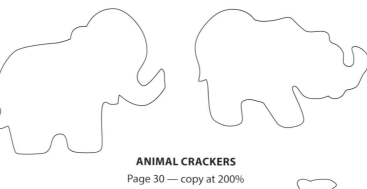

ANIMAL CRACKERS

Page 30 — copy at 200%

THRIFTED HOLIDAY TREES

Page 90 — copy at 400%

STRING OF STARS

Page 88 — copy at 200%

CHRISTMAS PINES Page 66

for small tree — copy at 165%

for medium tree — copy at 200%

for large tree — copy at 240%

base

STITCHED GIFT TAGS

Page 74 — copy at 200%

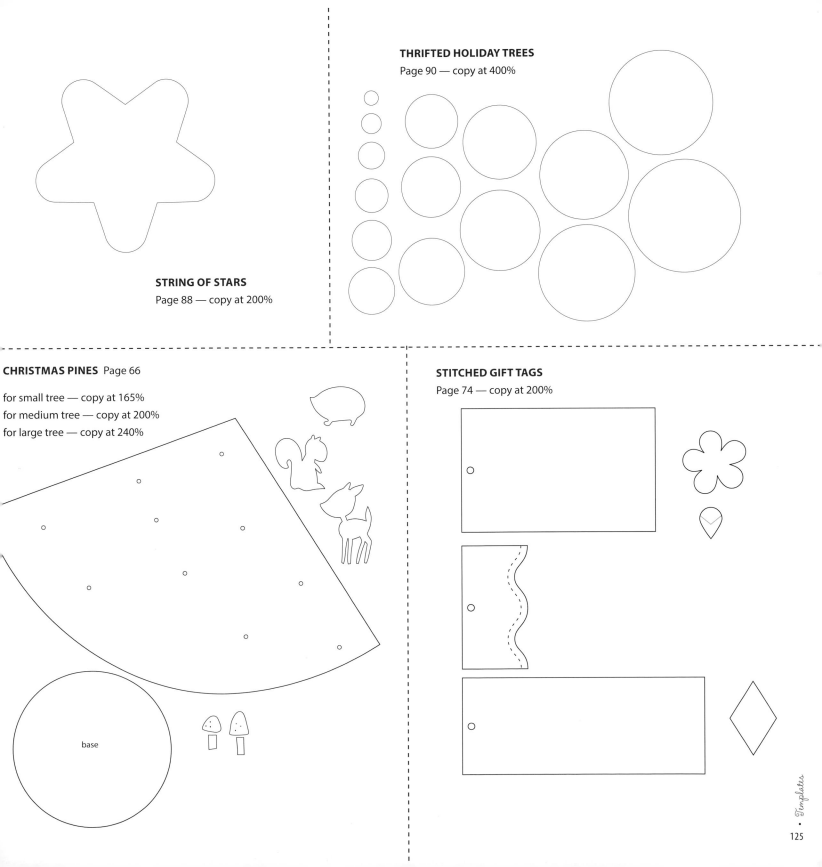

ABOUT *the* DESIGNERS

ELLEN LUCKETT BAKER

Ellen Luckett Baker is a mother and crafter who lives with her husband and two girls in Atlanta, Georgia. She holds degrees in art history and public administration with a focus in nonprofit management. In her pre-kids life, she worked as a floral designer, museum educator, and nonprofit fundraiser. Ellen's work has been featured in several publications. She is also the author of The Long Thread, a blog about handcrafted goods, online at www.thelongthread.com.

ESTHER COAR

Esther Coar has been married for 21 years and has seven children, ranging in age from four years to 17. A teacher turned stay-at-home mom, her schedule is full, but she always finds time to create and share her talents and projects with others. She's worked with felt for years, inspired by the fact that only simple tools are needed to create beautiful items from the material. Recently, she has used thrifted wool coats to create valances appliquéd with wool felt and simple embroidery. Her love of handwork comes from her Swedish grandmother.

CONSTANÇA CABRAL

Constança Cabral spends her days amongst fabrics and notions in her home studio in Lisbon, Portugal. A self-taught seamstress, she creates unique pieces for women and children alike. You can visit her daily blog, Saídos da Concha, online at saidosdaconcha.blogspot.com.

KAREN DE NARDI

Karen De Nardi, a designer from Adelaide, Australia, enjoys making jewelery and ornaments with felt and fabric. Characterized by its delicate style, her work is fun and color-savvy. Karen studied graphic design and is also a graduate of the Elder Conservatorium of Music. Although she began designing as a young girl, Karen has only recently ventured into the world of retail. Encouraged by her success at the local market, Karen decided to start her own online shop. Today, she stays busy meeting demands for her work from Australian retail outlets and customers around the world. You can find Karen's work online at www.denardi.etsy.com.

CATARINA FILIPE

Catarina Filipe, now based in Portugal, has been around buttons, threads, fabrics, and scissors all her life. With two seamstress step-grandmothers, beginning to sew at an early age was a natural step. She got her very own sewing machine at the age of eight. After many years without contact with needles and thread, she felt the urge to invest love and care in creating something with her own hands. Lately, Catarina works as a secretary and crafts in her spare time. She dreams of 72-hour days that would give her time to finish all of her creative projects.

CINDY GREY

Cindy Grey has lived her whole life in Wisconsin and calls Madison home. Retired, she spends as much time as possible at her cabin "up north" with her husband, Jim, and black lab, Molly. A few years ago during a spring blizzard, Cindy started making pincushions for friends and, as they say, the rest is history. She loves day trips, garage sales, flea markets, and antique stores. She's always looking for old sewing items to incorporate into pincushions and other projects. You can see more of her craftwork on her blog, Up the Creek Crafts, and purchase her work online at Up the Creek on Etsy.

CATHY GAUBERT

Cathy Gaubert is a wife, a momma, and a maker of things. Her days are filled with the antics of three sweet girlies, and the kitchen table is filled with more works-in-progress than you can shake a stick at. Her favorites include linen, wool felt, gingham, children's drawings, hand-stitching, fairy tales, forests, family, Clotilda Plantation, Neko Case, narwhals, kisses that have dance parties on her children's cheeks, flickr, quilts, gatherings at the tea party table, craft blogs, Creole tomato sandwiches, her mom's Bernina, and her husband. Peer into her world at handmadecathygaubert.blogspot.com, and do be sure to say hello.

LAURA HOWARD

Laura Howard is a self-taught crafter who grew up making things and has never stopped. She lives in Gloucester, England, in a small flat overrun with crafting supplies. Laura works mainly with felt and finds inspiration in its vibrant colors. A love of tea parties, English country gardens, and native British wildlife influences many of her designs. She has been selling her work online since 2007, and she writes about all her creative exploits on her blog, bugsandfishes.blogspot.com. Laura can be contacted via her website, lupinhandmade.com.

continued

ABOUT *the* DESIGNERS (continued)

LISA JORDAN

Lisa Jordan is an artist who's deeply inspired by nature. Whether she's sewing, felting, or tinkering with vintage buttons, the imprint of nature is evident in the colors, patterns, and textures she chooses. With a nod to sustainability, her work is largely crafted with recycled and natural materials. Reclaimed garment wool is one of her favorite mediums, and one she continues to explore. When she's not creating in her studio, she enjoys gardening, baking, and playing in Minnesota's lakes with her husband and four kids.

SUZIE MILLIONS

Suzie Millions is an artist, compulsive collector, and author of *The Complete Book of Retro Crafts* (Lark, 2009). She and her musician/artist/compulsive collector husband, Lance, live in an overstuffed cabin, complete with a walk-in Hank Williams shrine, in the woods of western North Carolina. Her paintings and shrines are shown and collected extensively. To see more work, or to contact Suzie, visit her website at www.suziemillions.com.

ULA PHELEP

Urszula (Ula) Phelep grew up in the "green lung" of Poland, in the Podlasie region. She moved to France nearly seven years ago to be with her love, Gwen, whom she met online. They live in the inspiring city of Nantes with their three-year-old lovely, Maïa. When not crafting, Ula works at the University of Nantes in the international relations office.

REBEKAH J. THOMPSON

Rebekah Thompson's early craft life was influenced by the old adage, "Necessity is the mother of invention." While growing up in a large family on a budget, she was encouraged to create instead of purchase. In Rebekah's adult life, a desire to create replaced necessity, and gave rise to expression of the ideas accrued during years of learning and dreaming. Love of the unconventional and handmade spurred her on to create unique items that intimately reflect her personality. Rebekeh created her own label of home décor items, which can be found in her online store at missmosh.etsy.com.

CATHY ZIEGELE

Cathy Ziegele, motivated by a scandalously naked troll doll, sewed her first felt caveman garment at age six. Her love of sewing grew from there. Cathy is now a retired executive chef whose past experiences include cooking for titans of industry in the yacht charter trade. The ease of working with felt was a nice departure from the chopping and dicing that was her life as a chef. She made clothes at first, but quilting was where she put her love of color to work. Many of her hand-sewn quilts are treasured gifts still in use today. Cathy's pincushions are available for purchase online at The Daily Pincushion on Etsy, and her digital scrapbooking designs can be found at www.theredporch.com.

Acknowledgments

First and foremost, this book would not exist without the brilliant ideas and guiding hand of Kathy Sheldon. Thank you so much, Kathy.

Thank you to the designers, for sharing your inventive projects and your enthusiasm for felt. You ladies are the best.

Thank you to Susan Wasinger, for the beautiful photography and design. Gosh, you're good.

Thank you, Mom (aka PamPam), for giving me…er…letting me borrow your sewing machine so many years ago.

Thank you to Billy Carestio, for all the design consultations and for putting up with our very messy kitchen table for so long.

Photo by Beth Sweet

About the Author

Editorial assistant with Lark Books by day and serial crafter all other times, AMANDA CARESTIO keeps herself busy with various stitching projects, linoleum block prints, and costume-oriented crafting pursuits (especially zombies and pirates). When she's not hunkered over her mother's old sewing machine, exploring the Blue Ridge Mountains, or out scootering the streets, Amanda enjoys spending quiet time with her design-star hubby and super-spoiled canine in Asheville, North Carolina. See more of her stitched creations in *Pretty Little Mini Quilts, Pretty Little Pillows,* and *Craft Challenge: Tea Towels* (all Lark, 2010) as well as online at digsandbean.blogspot.com.

Index

It's all on www.larkbooks.com

Can't find the materials you
need to create a project?
**Search our database for craft suppliers
& sources for hard-to-find materials.**

Got an idea for a book?
**Read our book proposal
guidelines and contact us.**

Want to show off your work?
Browse current calls for entries.

Want to know what new and
exciting books we're working on?
Sign up for our free e-newsletter.

Feeling crafty?
**Find free, downloadable
project directions on the site.**

Interested in learning more about
the authors, designers & editors
who create Lark books?